Silk Ribbon Embroidery 2

TRANSFORM YOUR CLOTHES

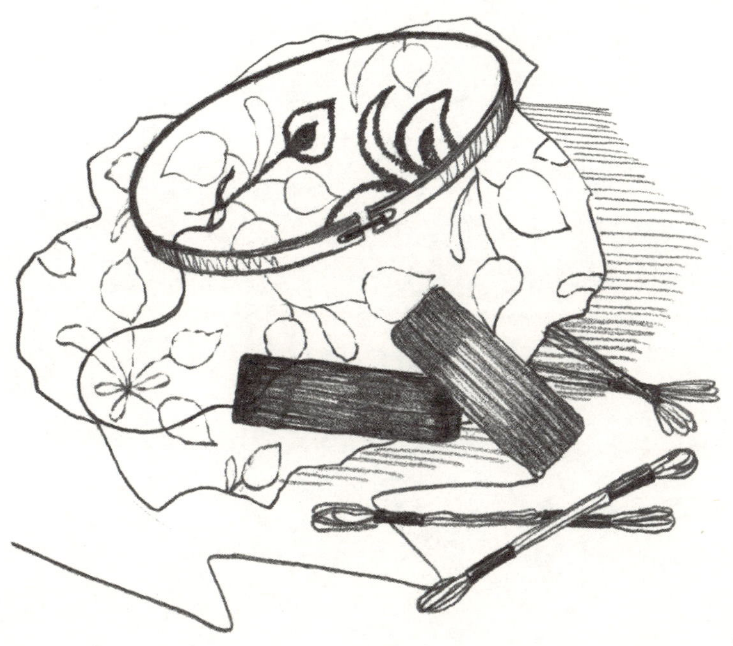

Silk Ribbon Embroidery 2

TRANSFORM YOUR CLOTHES

JENNY BRADFORD

GREENHOUSE

Greenhouse
Penguin Books Australia Ltd
487 Maroondah Highway, PO Box 257
Ringwood, Victoria 3134, Australia
Penguin Books Ltd
Harmondsworth, Middlesex, England
Viking Penguin, A Division of Penguin Books USA Inc
375 Hudson Street, New York, New York 10014, USA
Penguin Books Canada Limited
10 Alcorn Avenue, Toronto, Ontario, Canada M4V 1E4
Penguin Books (N.Z.) Ltd
182-190 Wairau Road, Auckland 10, New Zealand

First published by Greenhouse Publications Pty Ltd 1989
This edition by Penguin Books Australia Ltd 1990

10 9 8 7 6 5

Produced by Viking O'Neil
56 Claremont Street, South Yarra, Victoria 3141, Australia
A Division of Penguin Books Australia Ltd

Typeset by Meredith Typesetting
Printed in Australia by Impact Printing (Victoria) Pty Ltd

National Library of Australia
Cataloguing-in-Publication data

Bradford, Jenny.

Silk ribbon embroidery. 2. Transform your clothes.

ISBN 0 86436 241 2.
1. Embroidery. 2. Ribbon work. I. Title.

746.44

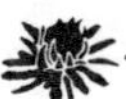 

Contents

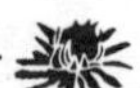

Acknowledgements

It is impossible to thank everyone who has either knowingly or unknowingly contributed to the ideas presented in this book.

I do however extend a big 'thank you' to the following people for their assistance: to Wendy Corke, Chris Bromfield and Neryl Richards who assembled some of the garments for me; to my son Terry for his help in preparing the manuscript and to my husband Don, whose ability to draw clear and accurate diagrams and patterns has made my task so much easier.

Jenny Bradford
1989

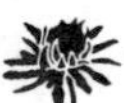
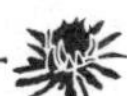

Introduction

The opportunity to acquire a new skill, or to enhance an old one, is something that most of us enjoy. Silk ribbon embroidery, as it is presented in this book, provides such an opportunity.

Those who have little or no experience in embroidery will find the stitches used in the designs are not difficult and the comparatively quick results gained by working with ribbon are quite exciting. For the experienced embroiderer working familiar stitches in a different medium can in itself be very satisfying and will, I hope, encourage experimentation with many other embroidery stitches which may be suitable for this type of work.

All the designs presented in this book have been worked using variations of six traditional embroidery stitches. These were selected for their suitability to create designs that will stand up to washing and wearing on everyday clothing. The same stitches combined with beads, metallic and other embroidery threads produce stunning surface decoration on garments and such things as belts and bags for special occasions.

Silk ribbon is soft and delicate and so I believe it to be ideally suited for embroidery on clothing. It is easy to achieve raised textured effects on delicate fabrics without adding weight and excessive bulk to the area chosen, a factor which can influence the look of the finished garment considerably.

 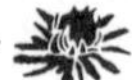

Materials

RIBBON

All the ribbon embroidery used for the designs in this book is worked with pure silk ribbon. It is available in two, four and seven millimetre widths. The ribbon is soft and pliable and it is used in the needle in the same way as any other embroidery thread.

Silk ribbon is available in a wide range of colours, the majority of which are colour fast and may be successfully washed, however care should be taken with the stronger shades as there can be some colour seepage onto pale background fabrics (see page 26).

There is now available a limited range of 4 mm polyester ribbon, almost identical in weight and texture to the silk ribbon. The advantages of this ribbon are that it is half the price of silk, colour-fast and it is less likely to snag or fray when being worked. It has more natural 'bounce' than silk and this can be a help, or a hindrance, depending on the stitches chosen and the type of design being worked.

My advice is that, if you can find a supply of this or any other types of ribbon of similar weight and texture, such as those woven into some of the more elaborate knitting yarns, it could be well worth experimenting with them.

NEEDLES

The choice of suitable needles will depend largely on the width of ribbon and the type of fabric chosen for the project.

Crewel, tapestry or chenille needles are all suitable:

- Crewel or embroidery needles have a sharp point, a short shaft and a long slender eye.
- Tapestry needles normally used for canvas work and cross stitch have a blunt point, short shaft and a long wider eye.
- Chenille needles have a sharp point, short shaft and a long broad eye.

When choosing a suitable needle for this, or any other form of embroidery, the following factors should govern your choice.

- The needle eye must accommodate the thread easily without creating too much friction which will cause the thread to deteriorate quickly.
- The needle should be just large enough to create a hole for the thread to pass through the fabric easily. Too small a hole will mean that you have to tug on the needle with every stitch but too large a needle will create unsightly holes in the fabric too large to be filled by the embroidery thread.
- The blunt point of a tapestry needle is designed so that it will not split the thread as it is worked. This can be a useful factor when working Portugese stem stitch or palestrina knot, where the needle is threaded under stitches already laid down on the fabric, but the blunt point must pass through the base fabric without causing pulled threads on the surface.

Suggested needle sizes

2 mm ribbon No 7 or 8 crewel, No 24 or 26 tapestry or chenille

4 mm ribbon No 6 crewel, No 24 or 26 tapestry or chenille.

7 mm ribbon No 20 chenille or tapestry.

Many of the designs incorporate some beads. There are special beading needles available but they are extremely fragile and not necessary for the type of beading involved here. I find a No. 9 or 10 straw needle the most satisfactory for this purpose.

THREADS

Almost any embroidery thread may be used in combination with the ribbon. It is largely a matter of personal choice and interpretation. The factors I take into consideration are whether the design will benefit from

- a dull or matt finish thread such as the cotton I have used to embroider stems and other highlights on the flower designs.
- a high lustre thread such as pure silk, Marlitt or metallic thread which adds to the richness of the silk (as used in the evening and bridal designs).

BEADS AND OTHER EMBELLISHMENTS

Beads of all shapes and sizes can be used with great effect to enhance ribbon embroidery and can do much to increase the impact of the design.

Ribbon work can be used to highlight applique designs or re-embroider designs on fabric or lace as illustrated.

FABRIC

Ribbon embroidery can be worked on almost any fabric suitable for garments. It may be necessary to stabilise knit fabrics with cotton voile, silk organza or batting to avoid stretching and puckering in the embroidered area.

Very fine or loosely woven fabrics will work up more evenly if a stabiliser is used. This also helps to prevent any back threads showing through on the front of the work.

To achieve a quilted effect it is possible to work the embroidery through a soft lightweight batting, which has been carefully tacked into place behind the surface fabric.

Watch for fabrics which may have a design suitable for re-embroidering. Once you start looking it is surprising to find just how many there are that are suitable. They are quick and easy to work and can be quite stunning (see skirt and top pictured).

Simple designs including abstract shapes, flowers, butterflies and so on can be used as applique designs on garments and then outlined and highlighted with embroidery and/or beads.

OTHER USEFUL EQUIPMENT

Marking pens There are several types available; transfer pencils, water soluble pens and fadable marking pens.

- A transfer pencil enables the pattern to be traced on to paper and then transferred to the fabric by ironing the tracing.
- A water soluble pen can be used to trace or draw the design onto the fabric. It is useful where lightweight fabrics enable a design to be traced through the fabric. The blue markings disappear when lightly sponged with cold water. Always use very light pressure when marking the fabric keeping the lines as fine and as light as possible and make sure you remove all traces of ink *before* ironing as heat sets the ink.
- Fadeable marking pens are great but markings can fade quickly. They are ideal for detailing the position of such things as flowers as you work. Do use markings as sparingly as possible, and preferably confine them to areas of heavy stitching, so that they will be covered anyway. For example use a single dot or circle to

mark the position of the centre of a flower rather than drawing the complete flower.

Embroidery frames There are many types of frames available and most of the projects in this book can be worked with or without a frame according to preference. See details of individual projects for further guidance.

Magnifying glasses I find a distressing number of students unwilling to admit that they really need glasses for fine handwork! Very few of us are lucky enough not to come across this problem at some stage of our lives.

Good lighting and clear vision are both essential for accurate work, they are also factors which have a direct bearing on how quickly we can work. For example, I see little point in spending precious minutes threading needles when good lighting and correct glasses will have the job done in a minute.

There are several types of magnifying glasses available, some are worn around the neck, some are free standing and others are combined with a lamp. Non-prescription magnifying spectacles are also available. Possible sources of supply are optical suppliers, chemists and needlework supply shops. Cost varies from a few dollars to hundreds of dollars for a top quality lamp/magnifyer combination, so the final choice of this type of equipment is probably dependant on how much one wishes to spend.

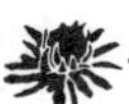
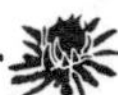

Embroidery with Ribbon

There is one major difference between using ribbon and thread for embroidery. The ribbon is flat whereas a thread is cylindrical. This means that it is necessary to ensure that the ribbon is manipulated to make it fold or twist in exactly the same way each time a stitch is worked. This ensures that the stitches look even.

It is not difficult to achieve uniformity of stitch size and tension, but it does require patience and perseverance. Some stitches require more manipulation than others.

The length of ribbon used in the needle may vary according to the stitch being worked. It is however worth remembering that due to the nature of the ribbon and the way in which it has to be manipulated, overworked and worn ribbon is much harder to handle. I therefore recommend using comparatively short lengths, a maximum of 30 cm (12 inches).

THREADING THE NEEDLE

The following method of threading the needle allows you to use every centimetre of ribbon and ensures that it does not slip out of the needle.

Thread the ribbon through the eye of the needle and, holding the end that has been threaded push the needle through the centre of the ribbon about 5 mm from the end. Pull back on the long end until the ribbon knots firmly on the eye of the needle. (Great too for threading ribbon or elastic through a casing using a large tapestry needle!)

THREADING THE NEEDLE

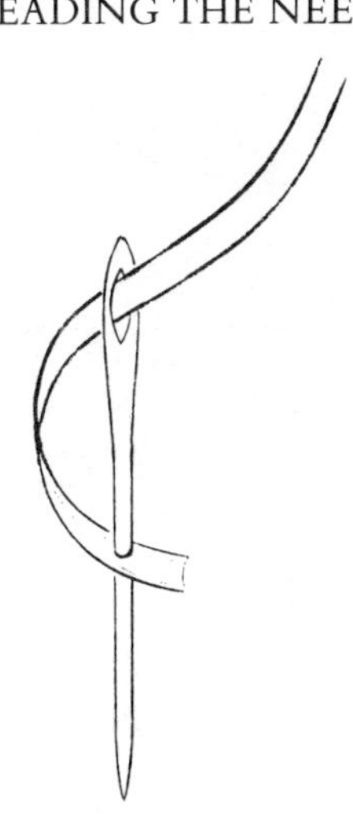

STARTING AND FINISHING

When starting a new area of work pull the needle through the fabric leaving a small tail at the back of the work then pierce this tail with the needle as the first stitch is completed. This will hold the ribbon firmly in place. Subsequent starting and finishing can be done by weaving the ribbon behind the stitches at the back of the work.

MANIPULATING THE RIBBON

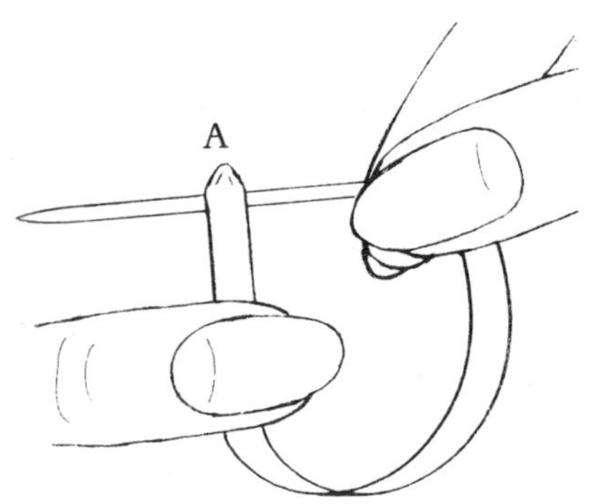

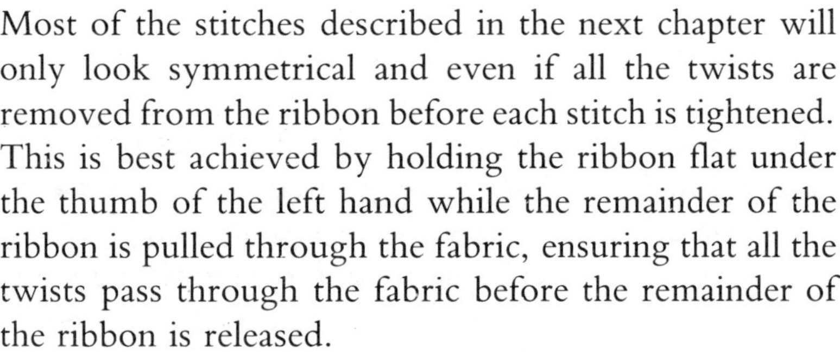
Most of the stitches described in the next chapter will only look symmetrical and even if all the twists are removed from the ribbon before each stitch is tightened. This is best achieved by holding the ribbon flat under the thumb of the left hand while the remainder of the ribbon is pulled through the fabric, ensuring that all the twists pass through the fabric before the remainder of the ribbon is released.

When working straight stitch it is necessary to *spread the ribbon* to ensure that it lies evenly as it comes out of the fabric.

This is achieved by holding the ribbon firmly under the left thumb and sliding the needle under the ribbon and back towards the exit point applying upward pressure on the ribbon with the needle. This should flatten the ribbon and ensure that the edges are not rolled over or under. Repeat if necessary. If the ribbon does not flatten correctly turn it over and repeat, it may have twisted as it passed through the base fabric.

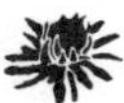

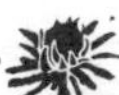

Stitches

The stitches described in the following pages have been chosen for their strength, durability and flexibility. Experienced embroiderers will undoubtedly have a range of stitches that are equally suitable and they may enjoy using some of their own personal favourites in designs.

Stitches requiring the ribbon to be firmly twisted or knotted will be the most satisfactory for everyday wear as there is less likelihood of the ribbon being pulled and snagged than with stitches where the ribbon is loosely looped on the surface.

The stitches are listed in order of difficulty. Before embarking on a project I suggest working a practice piece, trying out the stitches in various widths of ribbon to establish the tension and scale of the design.

STITCHES WORKED WITH SILK RIBBON

Straight Stitch

This is used for forget-me-nots, lily of the valley and ribbon and bead motifs.

- Bring the needle up at point A.
- Spread the ribbon (see previous page).
- Take the needle down at point B, making the stitch the required length.

  Ensure that all the twists are removed before the stitch is tightened (see previous page).

STRAIGHT STITCH

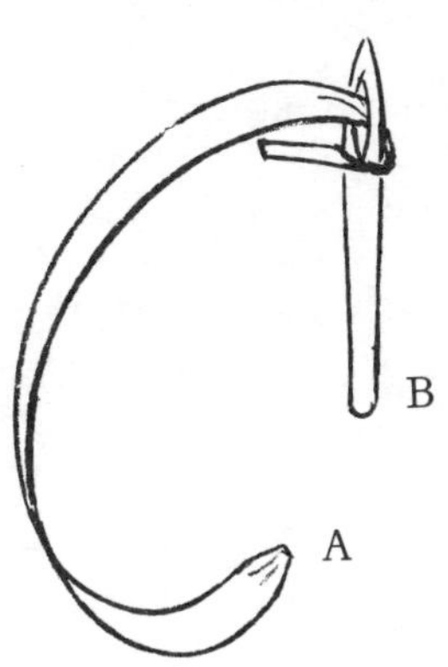

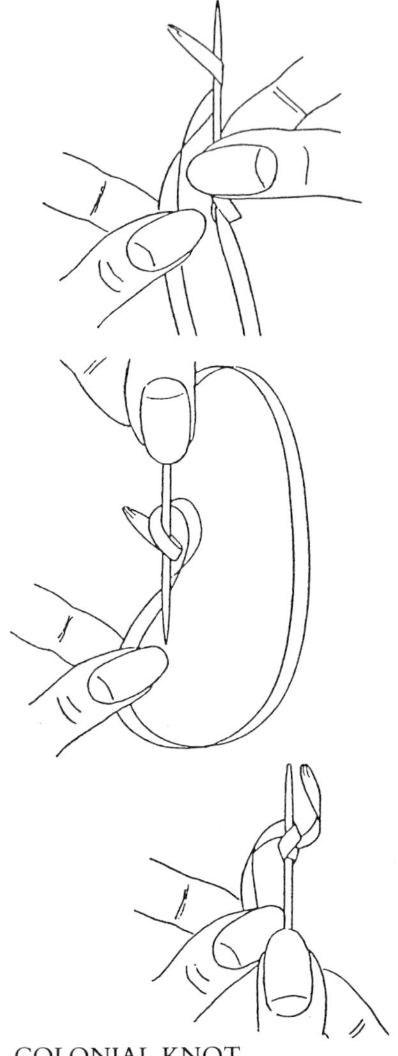
COLONIAL KNOT

Colonial Knot Also known as the candlewicking knot

This knot is particularly attractive when worked in ribbon; it is firmer than a French knot and it sits up well on the fabric. The ribbon is wound around the needle in the form of a figure eight keeping the full face of the ribbon flat on the needle at all times.

- Bring the needle up through the fabric and hold the ribbon between the thumb and first finger of the left hand about three or four centimetres away from the exit point.
- Imagining this exit point as a clock face, hold the needle pointing to twelve o'clock and pick up the ribbon from the left hand side on the point of the needle.
- Turn the needle anticlockwise (left) sliding it under the ribbon as it reaches six o'clock.
- Bring the needle over the top of the ribbon and turn it clockwise back to twelve o'clock and pass it back through the fabric close to but not through the original exit hole.

To produce well shaped even knots always neaten the ribbon around the shaft of the needle whilst the needle is held in a perpendicular position in the fabric and before completing the last step.

Twisted Chain

Traditionally used for borders and lines to create a textured look, this stitch works effectively in all widths of ribbon. As well as being used for this purpose in many of the designs given in this book, it is possible to work roses (page 21) and other flowers using this basic stitch.

- Work from the top of the design down directly over the line to be covered.
- Pull the needle through the fabric at point A.

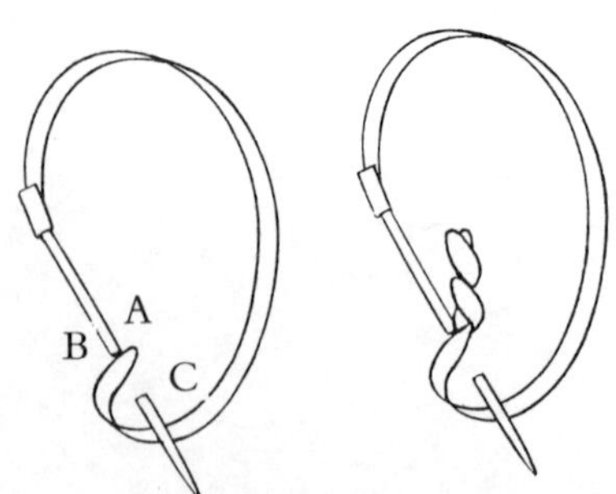

- Form a small anticlockwise loop of ribbon and pass the needle down through point B, level with, but to the *left* of, point A.
- Bring the needle back up at point C, inside the loop of ribbon, and immediately below point A. The distance between points A and C will depend on the thickness of the ribbon. It works well when this distance is equal to the width of the ribbon being used. To maintain even stitches the spacing between A to B and A to C must be constant with every stitch.
- Single twisted chain stitches can be worked as fill-in stitches or as flower petals. Each stitch is anchored with a tiny straight stitch at point C.

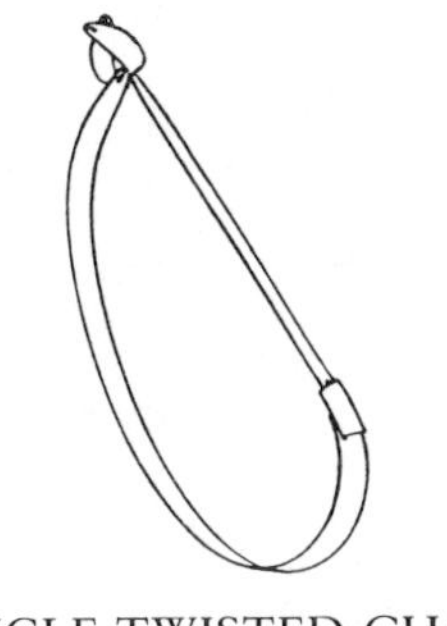
SINGLE TWISTED CHAIN

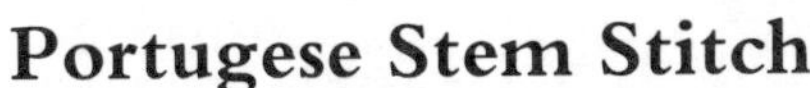

Portugese Stem Stitch

A lovely stitch with a cord like texture based on the more familiar stem stitch with which many readers will be familiar. If possible use a tapestry needle when working this stitch.

- Working from the bottom up and stitching directly over the marked design lines bring the needle up at point A.
- Keeping the ribbon on the right hand side of the needle take the needle down at point B and up again at C. The distances A to C and B to C should be equal and approximately the same as the width of the ribbon being used.
- With the ribbon *below* the needle pass the needle from right to left *between* the straight stitch just formed and the fabric, keeping the ribbon between B and C, step 2. Gently tighten the ribbon round the straight stitch, ensuring that it does not twist or curl.
- With the ribbon above the needle add a second wrap around the straight stitch below the first wrap and gently tighten as before.
- With the ribbon to the right of the needle work another stem stitch from D to B, step 4. Wrap as before

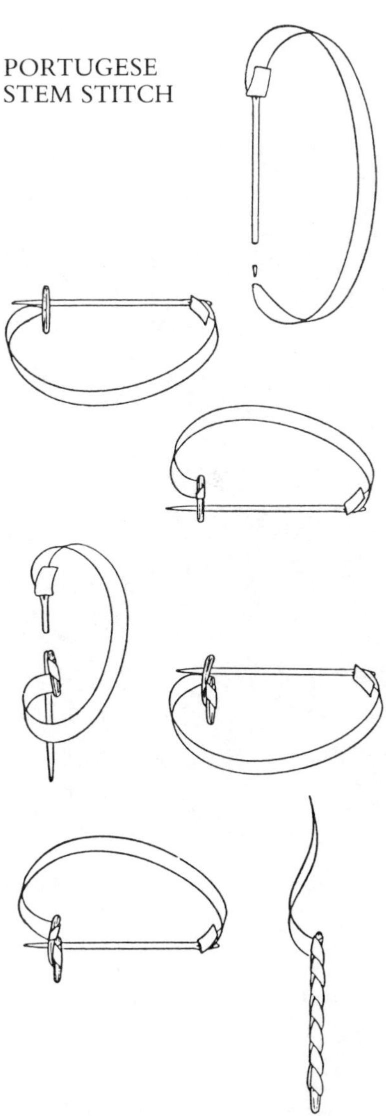
PORTUGESE STEM STITCH

taking the first wrap around the single stitch between D and B and the second wrap around both threads between B and C, step 6.

Be careful not to pick up threads from the base fabric or ribbon when wrapping the ribbon round the straight stem stitches. The use of a tapestry needle should help prevent this occurring.

Avoid twisting and curling the ribbon when wrapping the stem stitch in order to produce a flat cord like appearance to the stitch.

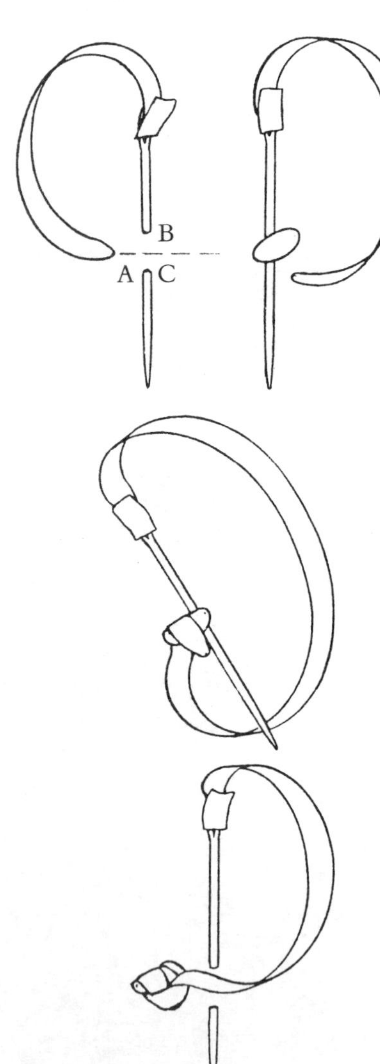

Palestrina or Double Knot Stitch

This attractive stitch originated in Europe and will be new to many. It is a hard wearing knotted stitch and is easy to launder.

- Working from left to right come up at point A on the line to be covered, take a small vertical stitch entering the fabric above the design line (B) and bring the needle out below this line (C), step 1. The distances between A to B and B to C should be equal and about the same as the ribbon width but the actual size will depend on the texture required.
- Keeping the thread to the right, slide the needle under the stitch formed from top to bottom and pull through, step 2.
- Holding the ribbon to the *left* and close to the stitches, loop it as shown and slide the needle under the original stitch a second time (above the loop just completed) and pull it through keeping the needle on top of the ribbon loop, step 3.

NB. Take care not to pick up threads from the base fabric when knotting the ribbon round the original stitch.

STITCHES WORKED WITH EMBROIDERY THREAD

Couching

An excellent stitch for stems and curved lines as it is easy to achieve a natural curve when working with two needles. Thread one needle with thread or cord of the required thickness. Thread a second needle with a single strand of matching embroidery thread.

- Using the heavier thread bring the needle up at point A and down at point B, bring it to the surface again at point C and leave this needle anchored in the fabric out of the way.
- Using the second needle anchor the main thread with tiny straight stitches at regular intervals curving the main thread as desired. Work a second stem from point C to D in the same manner.
  By using two needles the main thread can be shaped and adjusted as you work and the holding stitches are less obvious when worked in the finest possible thread.

TWIN NEEDLE COUCHING

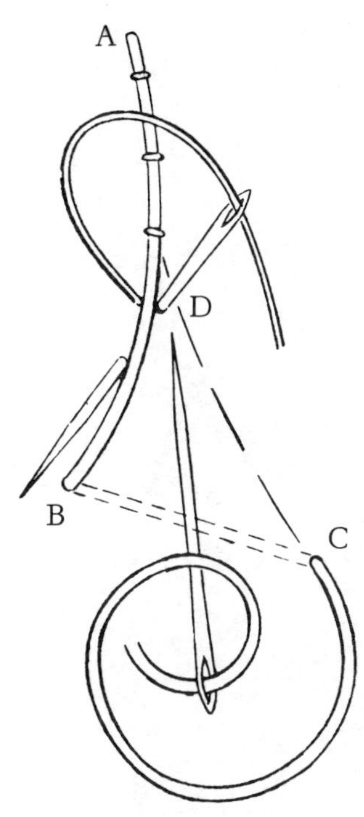

Lazy Daisy Stitch

- Bring the needle up at A, take it back down at A and out again at B looping the thread under the point of the needle.
- Pull the needle through the fabric tightening the thread gently. Anchor with a small stitch at the point of the stitch.

Satin stitch

This stitch is used to fill in areas such as the bodies of the butterflies on the windcheater. (Your satin stitch will be much more even if worked in this way instead of using 3 or 4 strands of thread at a time).

LAZY DAISY STITCH

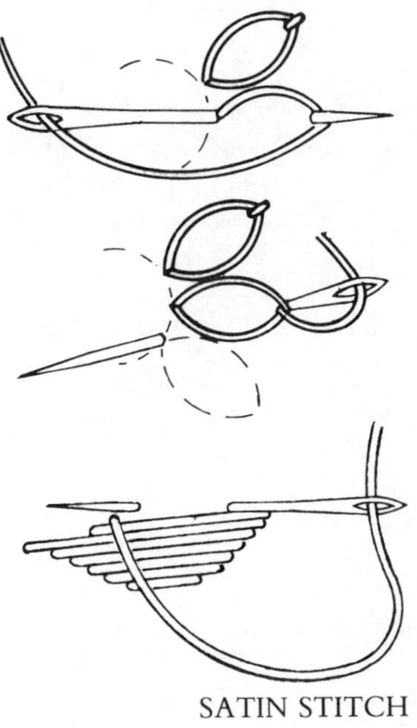

SATIN STITCH

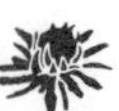

Creating with Stitches

Flowers (See page 48 for designs)

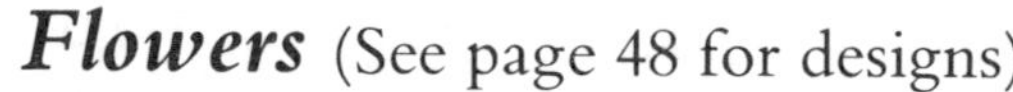

Forget-me-nots

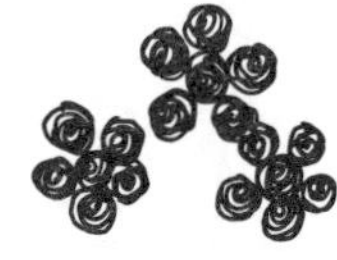

FORGET-ME-NOTS

Use colonial knots and 2 mm ribbon

- Work a single knot in yellow for the centre of the flower.
- Using blue ribbon work five knots around the centre knot as shown.

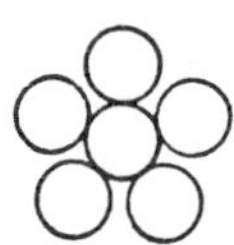

> If you have difficulty with spacing five petals on any flower imagine the centre as a clockface and position the five petals at 10, 12, 2, 5 and 7 o'clock or alternatively consider the centre as a body and give the body a head, two arms and two legs.

Lily of the valley

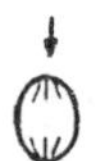

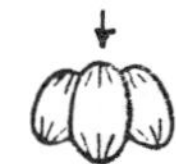

LILY OF THE VALLEY

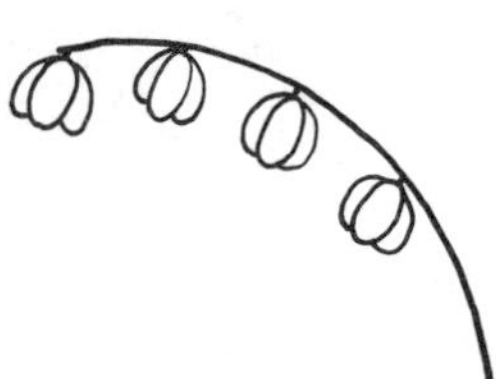

Use straight stitch and 2 or 4 mm ribbon, whichever width suits the scale of the flowers required.

The stitches should be approximately the same depth as the width of the ribbon being used.

- Work one straight centre petal in straight stitch.
- Work one straight stitch on either side of the first stitch sloping each stitch out slightly at the bottom of the bell shape as shown.
- Work a fourth stitch directly over the first centre stitch, taking care not to pull it too flat, giving the flower a bell shape.

Daphne

Straight stitch 4 petals, white or pink 2 mm ribbon.

Boronia

Straight stitch 4 petals, pink 2 mm ribbon.

Gypsophila or baby's breath

Straight stitch 5 petals, white 2 mm ribbon.

All these flowers are tiny and so they are normally worked with 2 mm ribbon to maintain proportion.

- Mark a tiny dot on the fabric to position the centre of the flower.
- Work four or five straight stitch petals around the dot (see previous page for five petal placement).
- Work a small colonial knot in stranded cotton (2 strands) for the centre of each flower.

- NB. Spread the ribbon as you work each stitch holding the ribbon in line with, but away from, the direction in which the stitch will lie when it is completed.

Roses

Twisted chain and colonial knot. Use 3 shaded colours of ribbon.

- Use 2 or 4 mm ribbon, according to the size required.
- In the darkest shade work a colonial knot for the centre of the rose.
- Using the middle shade work three or four twisted stitches in a neat circle around the knot.
- With the lightest shade work a second circle of five or six twisted chain stitches so that it touches but does not overlap the previous stitches.

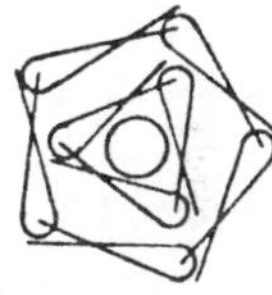

ROSE STITCH PLACEMENT

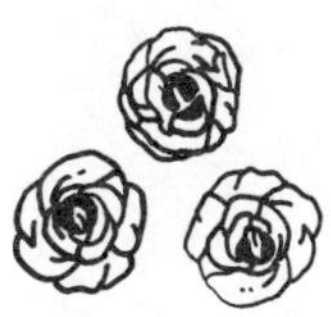

Rose buds

Method 1 Use colonial knot and straight stitch.

- With 2 or 4 mm ribbon, according to the size required, work a single colonial knot at the top of the bud.
- Work two straight stitches from a common base point. Start them at about a ribbon's width distance from the edge of the colonial knot and finish them

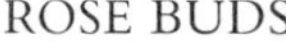

ROSE BUDS

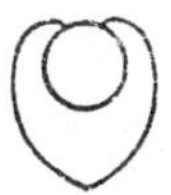

METHOD 1

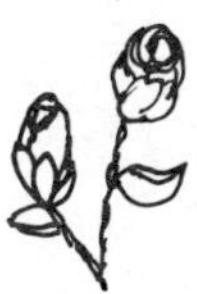

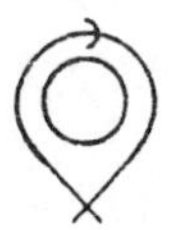

METHOD 2

one on each side of the knot at about eleven o'clock and one o'clock positions. Angle the needle in towards the centre line under the knot.

Method 2 Use colonial knot and twisted chain. Work as described in *Method 1*, substituting a single twisted chain stitch for the two straight stitches.

BEADED FLOWERS

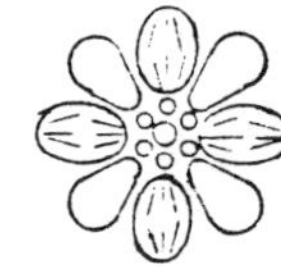

BEAD FLOWERS

A combination of beads and silk ribbon petals have been used in some designs. It is best to work these flowers from the centre out, as it is difficult to judge exactly how much room is required to position the beads.

Examples in this book are the pearl and silk flowers on the bridal bag and the bugle bead and silk flowers on the black evening bag. Both examples of flowers were constructed in the same way. Commence by sewing on a single seed bead for the very centre of the flower, encircle this bead with five or six more seed beads, sewing them firmly and very close together. Take four or six bugle beads or teardrop shaped pearls and sew them at equal intervals with the base touching the centre circle as shown. Work silk ribbon straight stitch petals in the spaces between the beads. Use 4 or 7 mm ribbon for larger flowers. Smaller flowers can be worked using a single bead for the centre and shorter bugle beads for the petals.

BOWS

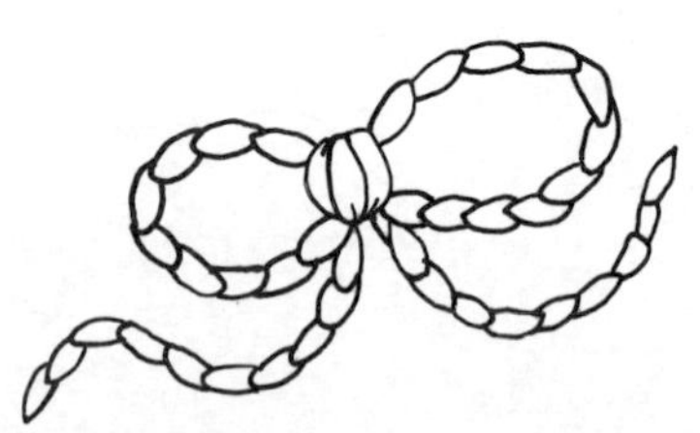

Very pretty bows can be worked using twisted chain stitch. Trace or draw freehand the required design with a fadable pen. Work twisted chain in 2 or 4 mm ribbon. Cover the centre 'knot' with one or two straight stitches.

APPLIQUE

There are many different ways of approaching applique work and it is not my intention to deal in any great detail with these here as there are many excellent books available on the subject.

Recently I have become familiar with the method used on the projects in this book and it is certainly very quick, easy and successful so I recommend that you try it.

The picture is built up by working from the back of the work in such a way that it enables reproduction of very fine detail in the applique design. Small intricate shapes cause no problems using this method. If you have not already done so try using some of the excellent machine embroidery threads now on the market for this type of work. They produce a beautiful satin stitch far superior to regular sewing thread.

Materials required

- A design for applique. Start with a simple design and avoid patterns with too many pieces, sharp corners and tight curves (see pages 46 and 47).
- Fabric for the applique design.
- Fabric for the project to be worked on. It is much easier to work on a flat piece of fabric to be made up after the applique is completed.
- Matching or contrasting thread for the applique fabrics.
- Backing fabric such as adhesive bonding fabric if desired.
- Paper onto which the reversed design is traced. (I find computer paper is ideal as it comes in a useful size, it is strong and of an ideal weight.)

Method Trace the chosen design very carefully onto the paper. Note that because the design is to be placed on the wrong side of the work the design will be reversed.

If you are using an adhesive bonding fabric bond it onto the fabrics required for applique.

Start with the section of the design that will be the back piece. Cut a generous sized piece of the applique fabric allowing plenty of clearance around the edges of the design.

Pin it to the right side of the garment. With the *wrong* side of the garment uppermost and using a straight stitch, sew around the outline of the selected piece through the paper and fabrics. Make sure you carefully follow the line drawn on the paper. Note that the smaller the stitch length used the easier it is to negotiate curves.

Remove the work from the machine and trim the applique very carefully back to the machine line using small sharp scissors. Satin stitch over the edges from the front.

Working piece by piece build up the design sewing along the lines on the paper each time.

When the design is finished carefully tear away the backing paper.

Complex designs will need careful planning to ensure the correct order in the layering of the fabrics. It will be necessary to satin stitch certain areas before proceeding with each layer to create a neat finish and correct perspective.

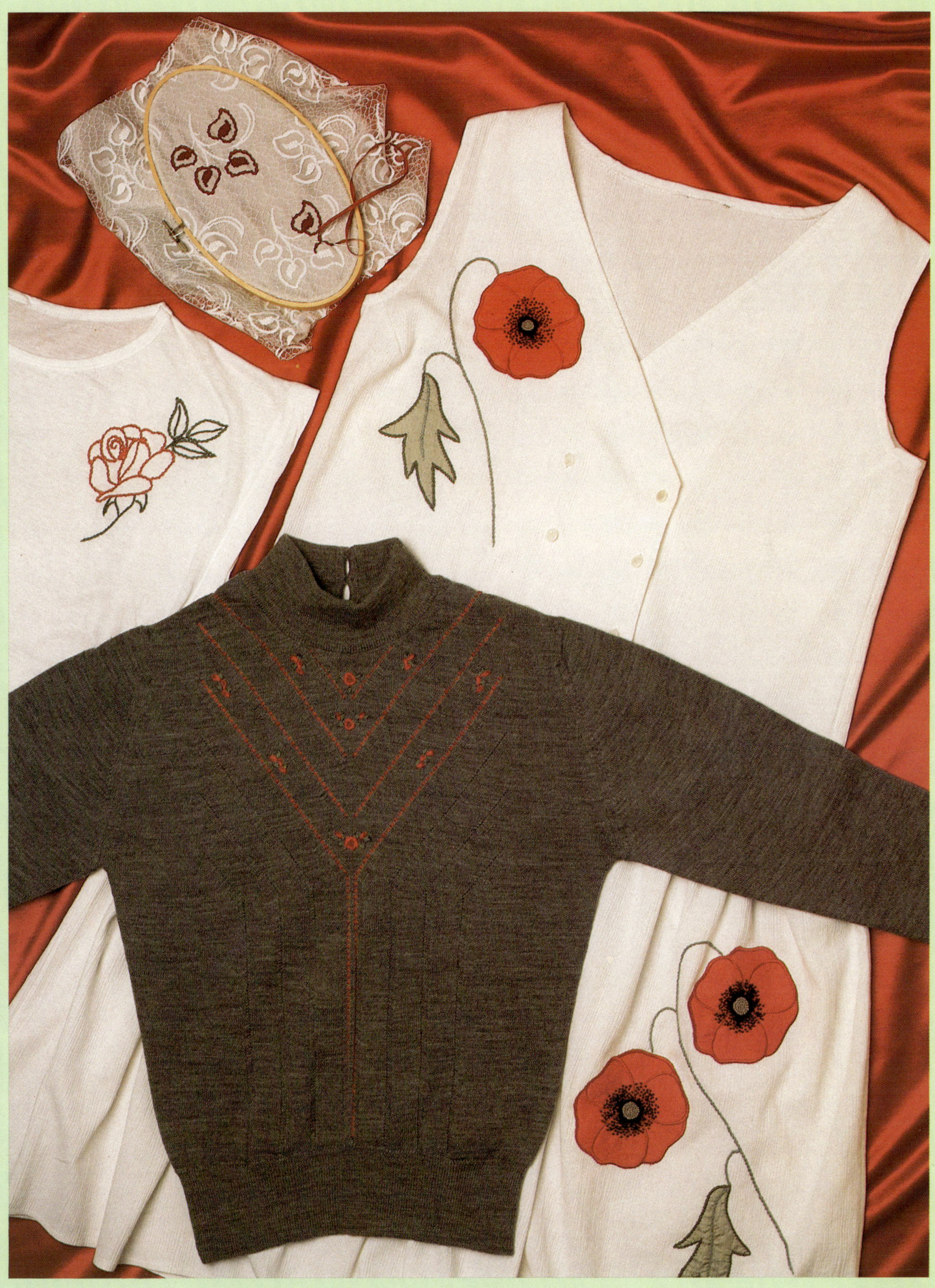

Ready made clothes can be dressed up with embroidery and applique that will withstand everyday wear

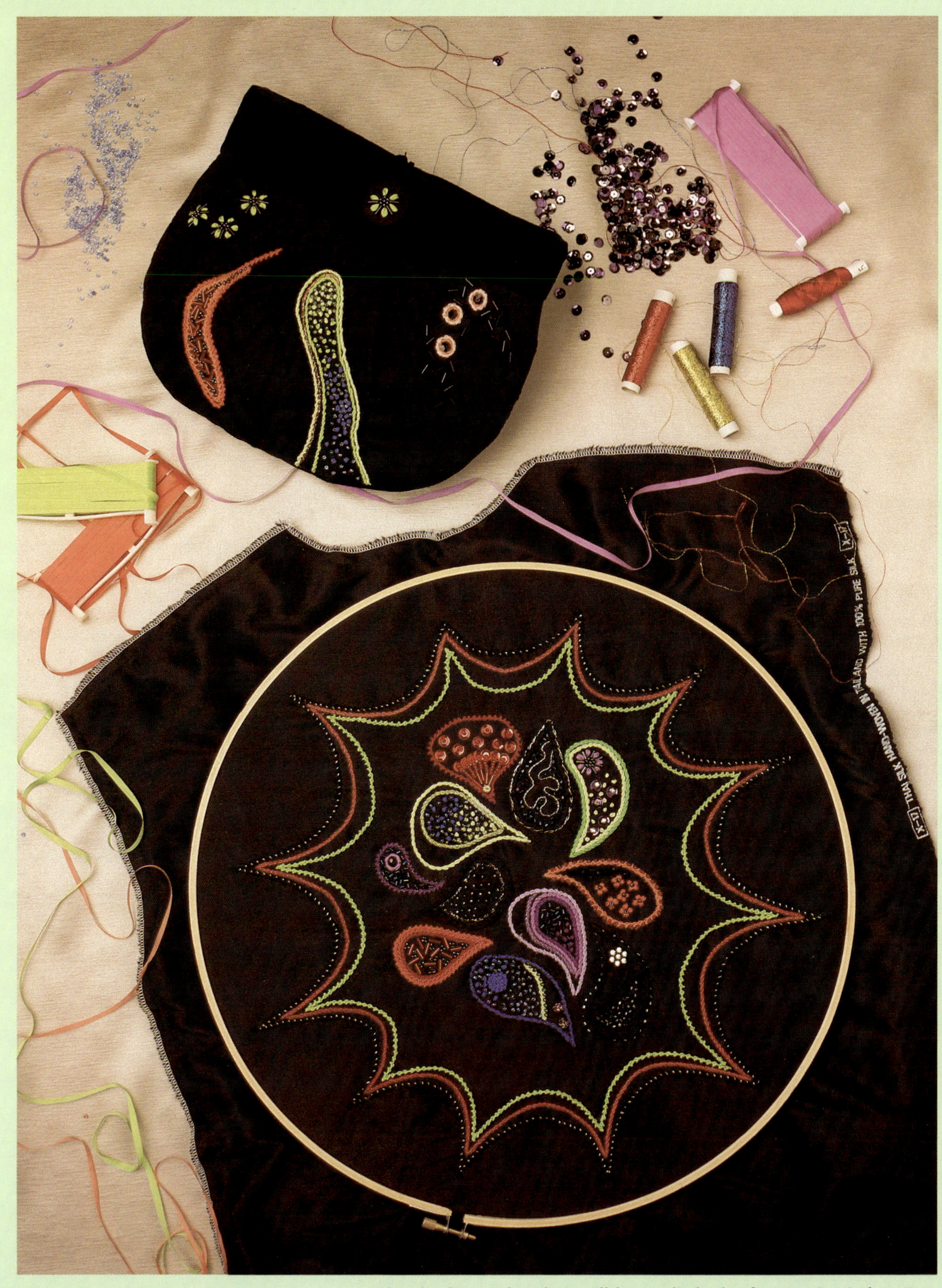

This dazzling embroidery will be on the back of an evening jacket. Embroidery on the back or front yoke area will stand out best

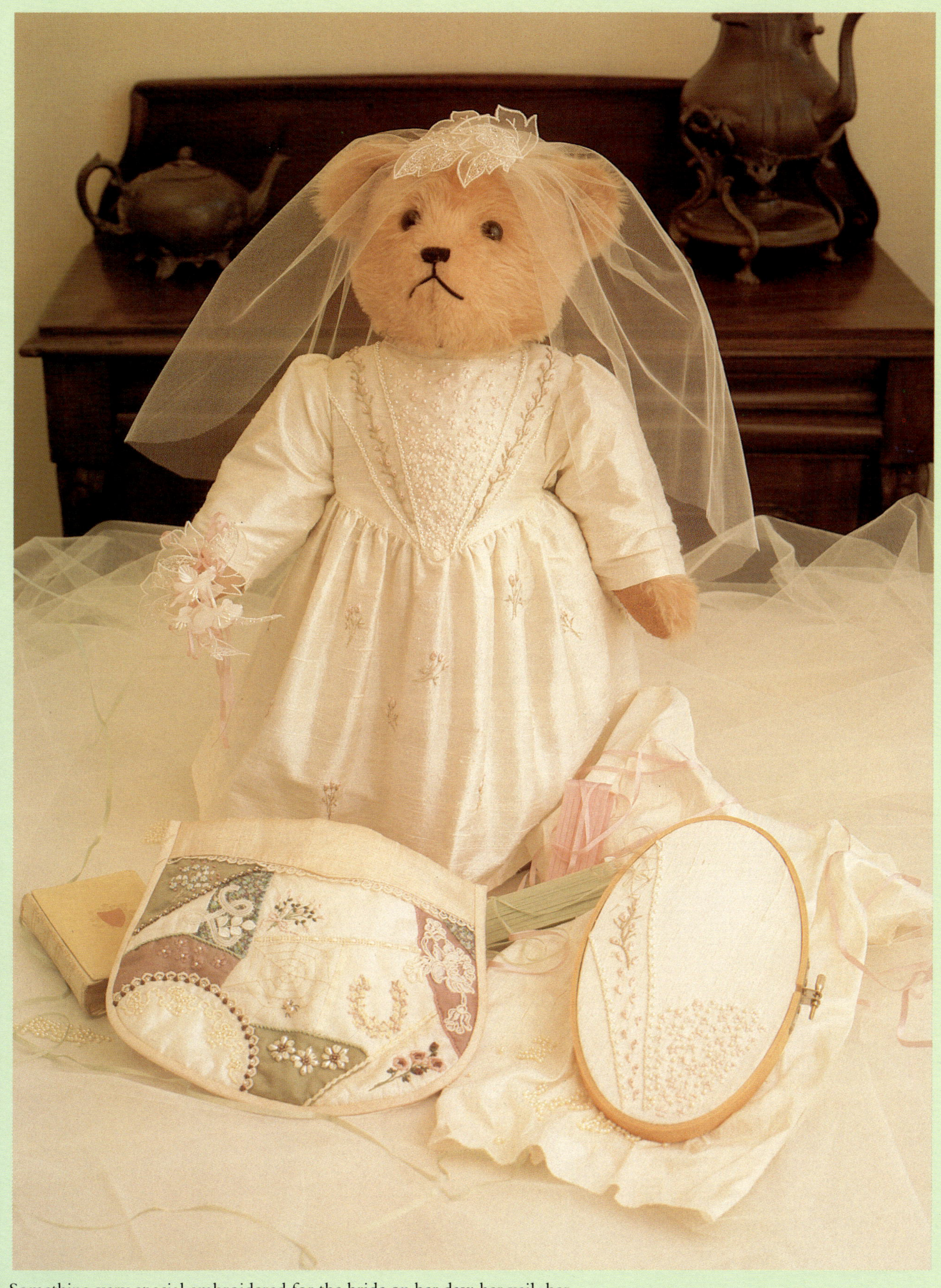

Something very special embroidered for the bride on her day; her veil, her bodice or the little keepsake bag

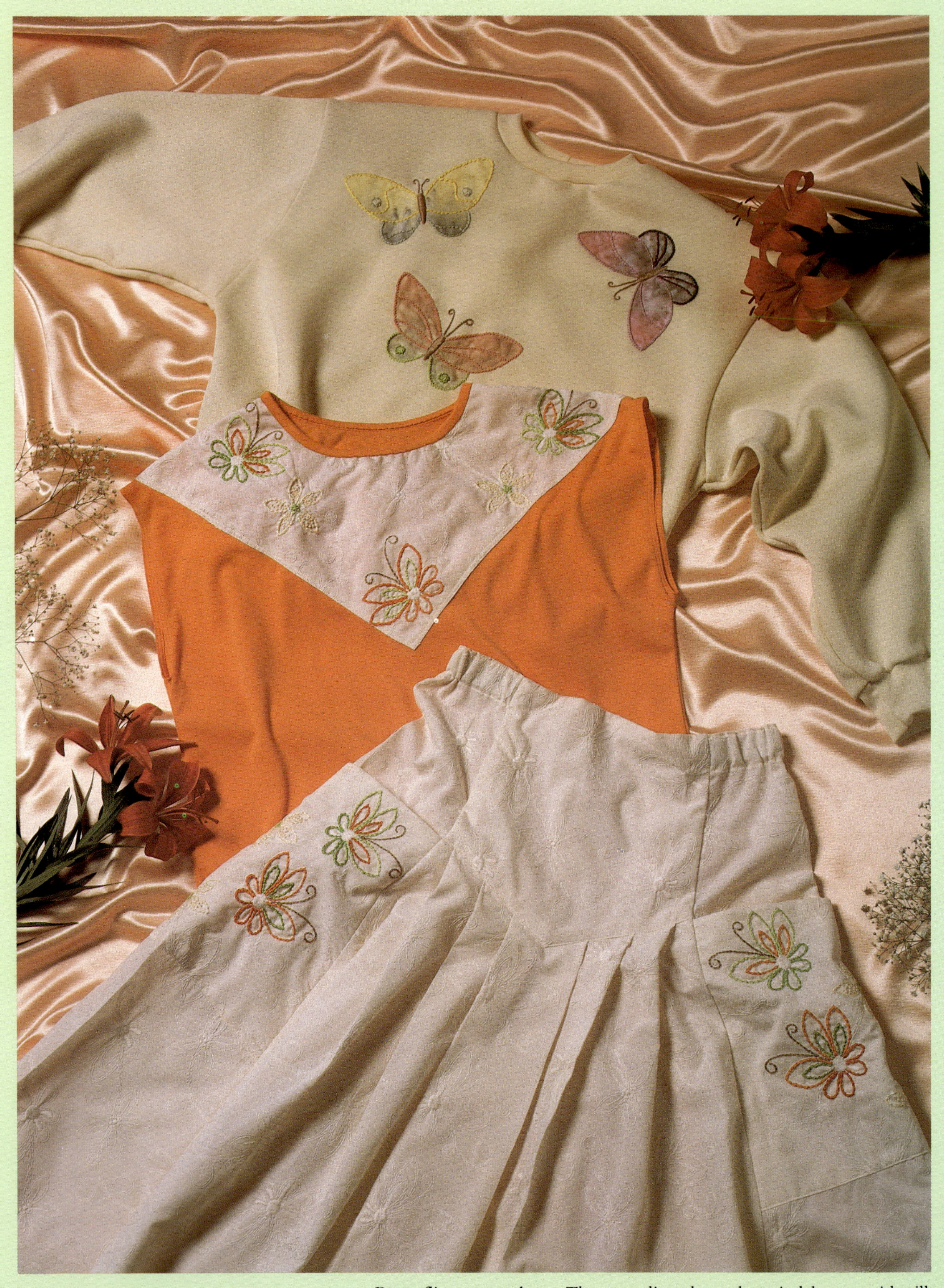

Butterflies everywhere. Those appliqued on the windcheater with silk ribbon have a lovely gauze texture. The skirt and top show how re-embroidery enhances fabrics and garments

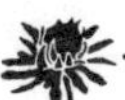

Planning a Project

Most of us are familiar with the frustration of making something that turns out to be 'not quite right', but careful planning will certainly reduce the chances of failure.

Start with consideration of the end product. What style of garment will suit the occasion? What type of fabric is suitable for that style? What type of embroidery will complement the garment? For example, very elaborate embroidery looks great on evening wear but may be totally out of place and impractical on a T-shirt or everyday dress.

As mentioned previously some of the stronger colours in the silk ribbon are not colour fast to hand washing. It is therefore not practical to put scarlet embroidery on a white blouse, the better choice would be soft colours on pastel backgrounds but strong colours will be fine on dark background fabrics.

All the stitches described in this book will launder satisfactorily. However, if you experiment with other embroidery stitches, remember that firmly woven knotted stitches have harder wearing properties than loopy stitches.

Silk ribbon is very light and should not affect the way any fabric hangs or drapes but beads are heavy and require that the fabric is heavy enough to support the embroidery without distorting the shape of the finished product.

When incorporating beads into a design be careful

not to sew them too close to a seam line so that there is clearance for the machine foot. If necessary use a zipper foot when constructing that part of the project.

Fabrics that are to be washed after assembly should be washed before starting the project. I do not however recommend washing silk ribbon before it is used for embroidery as it loses much of its body, making it more difficult to work and manipulate.

CARE OF EMBROIDERED GARMENTS

Some silk ribbon carries a care instruction label recommending 'dry clean only'. This method should certainly be adopted if there is any danger of colour leakage from dark colours used in the embroidery. Be sure to inform the cleaning company that silk is involved and request special care be taken with both the type of cleaning fluid used and the pressing afterwards. Beads may also require special consideration.

Everyday garments can be washed in the washing machine using a mild soap solution rather than a strong detergent which may cause colour fading in some cases.

Glass beads wash satisfactorily but some of the more elaborate beads, including those that are silver or gold lined, are not recommended for washing.

I always sew on each type of bead with a separate thread so that it is possible to renew any one type, without all the others being disturbed, should it be necessary.

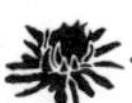

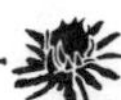

Projects and Designs

As can be seen from the wide variety of garments shown in this book silk ribbon embroidery is very effective and can be used in many different ways.

All the garments illustrated and detailed in this book are made from commercially available patterns.

When choosing a pattern care should be taken to ensure that seams and darts do not conflict with the design you intend working on the garment. Inspiration for designs can often be drawn from illustrations in pattern books, fashion magazines, embroidery, patchwork and quilting sources. Do not forget the craft and accessory section of the pattern books as these often contain ideas for collars, bags and belts. Children's colouring books are an excellent source of simple designs that may be used for applique work.

BLOUSE

The blouse pictured on the front cover is made from high quality lawn. The embroidered design (see page 28) is simple but effective and can be used in a variety of ways from a single spray, used on the blouse cuffs, to multiple repeats to form a panel or border. This design would be easy to work on a ready made garment, but otherwise I recommend working the embroidery before the garment is made up.

Small embroidered sections such as collar or cuffs will be easier to handle if they are *not* cut out prior to embroidery. Draw the outline of the pattern piece onto the fabric so as to position the embroidery accurately and remember to reverse the pattern when working matching cuffs and yokes etc.

The original design was worked using twisted chain stitch for the flowers and Portugese stem stitch for the leaf and stem. Flower centres may be beaded, as in the original, or worked in colonial knots.

BLOUSE PATTERN

RE-EMBROIDERED SKIRT AND TOP

This outfit was planned around the fabric; a perfect example of how ribbon embroidery can be used to build on the original design of the fabric to create a really individual piece. This method of approach would be ideal for those who find the mere mention of 'original design' too terrifying to contemplate.

For those more confident and eager to work on

their own designs a similar effect can be achieved by quilting or sewing a simple design onto the fabric using matching thread and a twin needle then re-embroidering the outline with ribbon. Designs used for quilting can be used as a basis for this type of work. Use a long stitch and a heavier top stitching thread for added texture. To achieve a quilted effect thin batting can be used either before or after the initial sewing process.

The amount of embroidery used on garments of this type is totally a matter of taste and may vary from a single motif to the whole garment.

The re-embroidery illustrated is worked in twisted chain using three shades of 4 mm ribbon for each butterfly. The feelers are couched silk cord. Flowers are outlined in twisted chain using 4 mm ribbon, with a mixture of colonial knots and straight stitches used for the centres and inner half of the petals.

EMBROIDERED PULLOVER

This decoration is worked on a purchased pullover. In the pullover illustrated 2 mm ribbon is threaded through rows of holes that occur in the basic design accentuating that part of the design. Ribbon roses and rosebuds are used in the yoke area to add further embellishment.

When working on a garment of this type take care that the embroidery does not restrict the stretch of the garment when it is being worn. Unsightly distortion may occur if the embroidery is pulled too tight. Make sure that you finish embroidery ribbons and threads off neatly behind each area of embroidery; never 'jump across' when moving from one area to another. Small individual motifs of embroidery are less likely to cause distortion than one large motif.

WEDDING DRESS BODICE

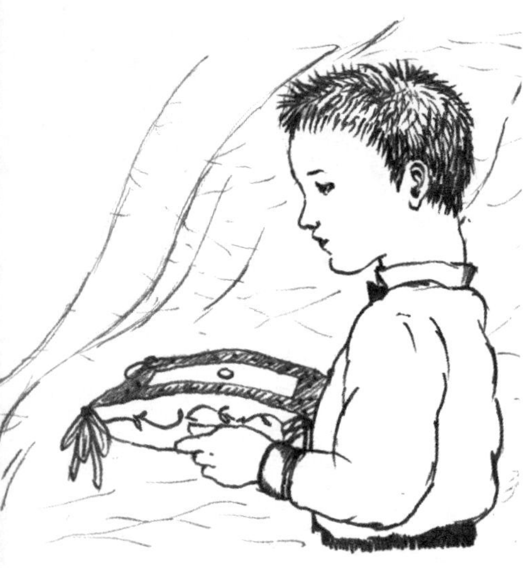

Silk ribbon embroidery is I feel particularly suitable for this type of garment. It can be used in many different ways to give a personal touch to garments and accessories for that very special day.

The possibilities of this type of work are limitless from scattering a few dainty rosebuds on the bodice or skirt of a gown to richly embellishing the whole bodice, panels of the skirt and the sleeves.

The design on the teddybear wedding gown uses palestrina knot for the line work and, to decorate the centre panel, straight stitch flowers with colonial knot centres. Rosebuds trail down the side panels. The embroidery is highlighted with tiny seed pearls scattered between the flowers on the centre panel and sewn between each stitch on the rows of palestrina knots. Palestrina knot is excellent for this as the beads sit neatly between each stitch.

When using a frame for embroidery do not sew on beads until all embroidery is finished as the beads will prevent the work from being moved in the frame.

Head-dresses, veils, ring pillows and wedding favours are all ideal projects to show off this beautiful form of embroidery.

The clutch purse pictured, made from fabrics used for wedding outfits worn by the bridal party, would be a treasured keepsake for the bride or her attendants. The bag is made from crazy patchwork embellished with silk ribbon embroidery and beads.

The embroidery must compliment the chosen design for the wedding gown. Whether floral or abstract designs are preferred, placement of the embroidery should enhance the lines of the overall design rather than detract from them.

A safe guideline to follow is to highlight the key design points of the style. Examples are working around a neckline, embroidering a high collar, cuffs and large decorative bows.

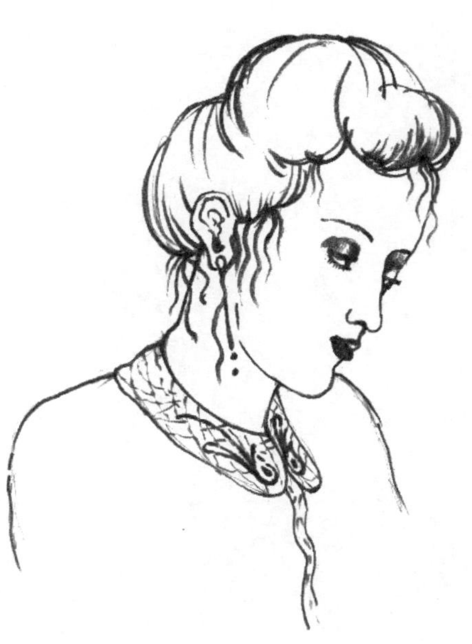

RE-EMBROIDERING LACE

The choice of pattern in the lace for this type of work is important. I find a clear simple design is best. Complicated patterns are difficult to work and the embroidery does little to enhance the project if you are outlining the design. However flower centres may be highlighted to great effect on some of the fussier designs.

Colour choice is very personal, however I find that a soft contrast between the lace and background fabric is much more pleasing than a strong colour contrast.

APPLIQUED MOTIFS

This type of work is suitable on clothing for people of all ages. The butterfly windcheater and poppy dress are two good examples.

The method of applique described on page 23 is equally successful using plain or knit fabrics. Where the applique shape is to be outlined with silk ribbon do not use heavy satin stitch over the trimmed edge. Zigzag carefully around the trimmed edge using a narrow open stitch then work the embroidery stitches over the edge from one side of the stitching to the other. This will ensure that the machine stitching is hidden under the ribbon.

Twisted chain and palestrina stitch work perfectly using the needle placement already described (see pages 16 and 18).

To work Portugese stem stitch angle the needle between points B and C so that they are on the opposite sides of the machine stitching.

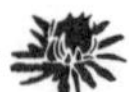

Floral Designs

In both designs illustrated the five petal flowers on the front cover and the six petal poppy, the leaves are outlined with Portugese stem stitch using 2 mm silk ribbon. The flowers are satin stitched with machine embroidery thread grading the width of the satin stitching as it moves towards the centre of the flower. The flower centres are worked in colonial knots using 2 or 4 mm ribbon interspersed with tiny seed beads if desired.

Butterfly Windcheater

All the butterflies for this design were cut from a piece of hand dyed cotton fabric. Careful placement of the design was made to maximise the lovely shading in the wings of the butterflies. The colours were softened by using a layer of off white silk organza over the top of this fabric. Both these layers of fabric were appliqued simultaneously, using the method described on page 23. The butterflies are outlined and highlights embroidered using 2 or 4 mm ribbon and a selection of stitches as desired. The bodies are worked in satin stitch.

T-SHIRT WITH ROSE

Simple outline designs are quick and easy. Backing the design with fine voile when working on knit fabric helps to avoid any distortion.

Line designs may be traced from book illustrations, children's colouring books, applique and quilting designs.

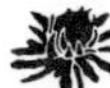

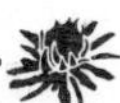

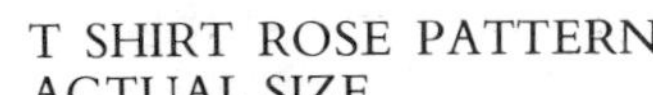

T SHIRT ROSE PATTERN
ACTUAL SIZE

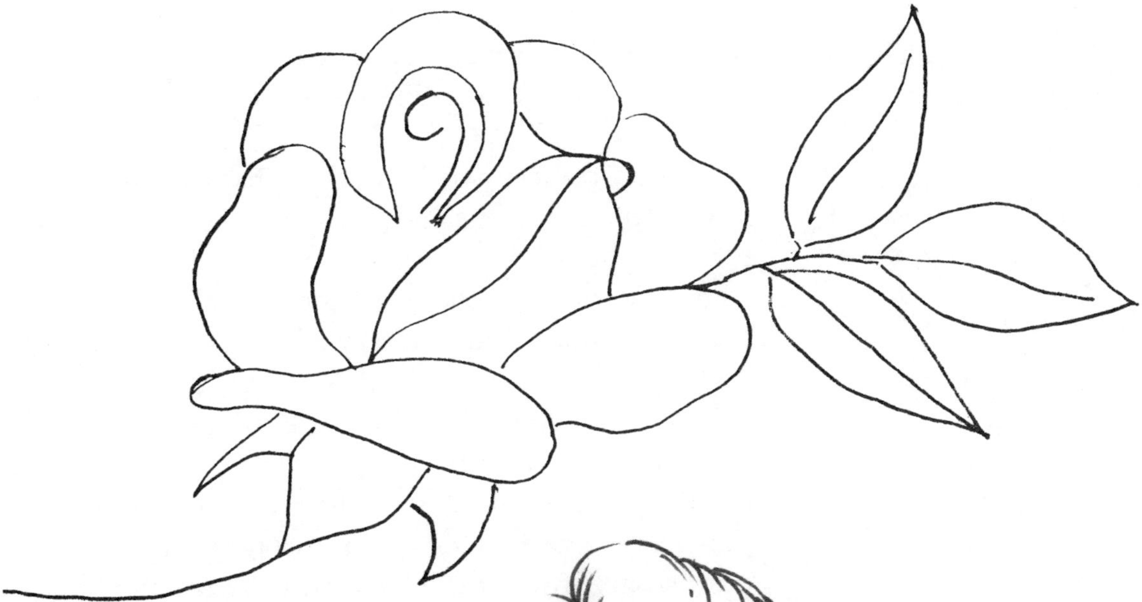

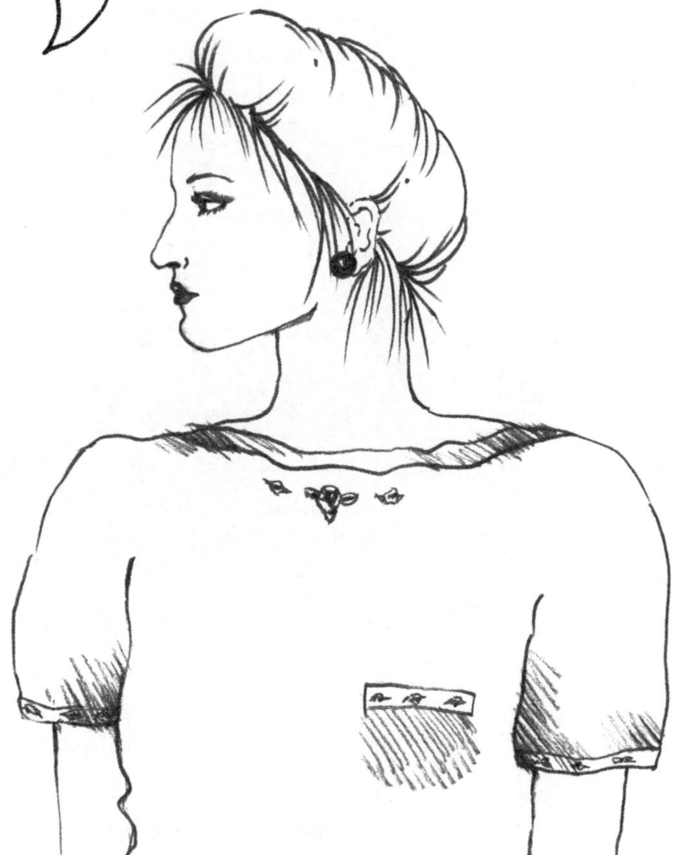

EVENING JACKET OR VEST

The design illustrated has been worked on pure silk, backed with lightweight quilt batting, and embroidered with a mixture of silk ribbon, silk thread, metallic thread, and beads.

Embroidery worked on the back or yoke area of any garment will be more noticeable than that which is worked on the lower edge, cuffs or pockets. The use of bright colours will attract the eye whereas the use of blended colours, close to that of the background colour will achieve a more classic style and often needs a second look to fully appreciate the work involved.

To reproduce the design for the jacket enlarge the outline pattern given overleaf using graph paper. Trace the shapes from pages 35 and 38 positioning them by number according to the diagram. Alternatively photocopy/enlarge the diagram to achieve full size.

Transferring hand drawn designs onto fabric can be a problem particularly on dark backgrounds. The design for the jacket back was drawn onto computer paper then marked onto the jacket back by machine using the applique method described on page 24. Use machine embroidery thread in a matching colour and a long length stitch instead of the small stitch length recommended for applique work. The stitches will be well hidden under the embroidery or can easily be removed as you work.

Transferring a design onto light background fabric may be done by drawing the design onto paper using a dark heavy line. Tape the design to a window, position the fabric right side up over the design and hold or tape in place. Trace the design onto the fabric using a water soluble or fadeable pen.

Evening Jacket Embroidery

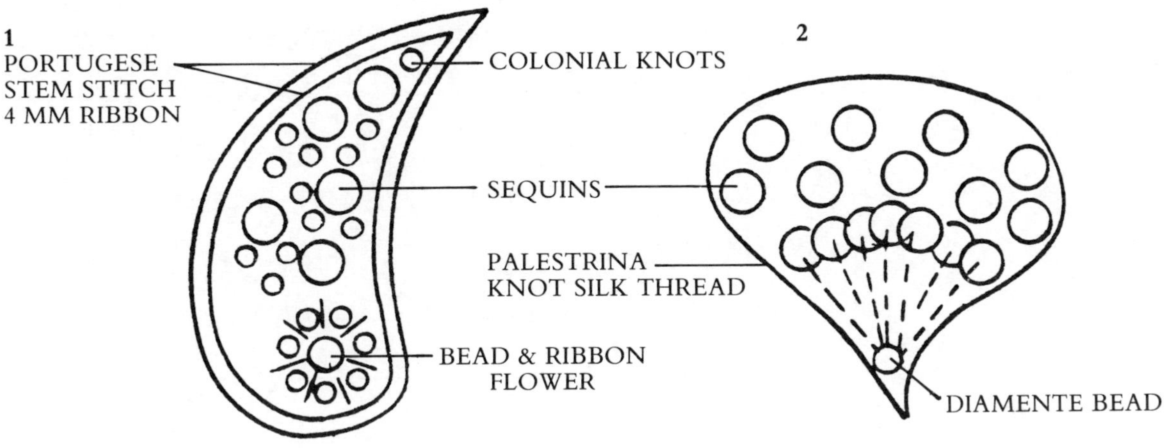

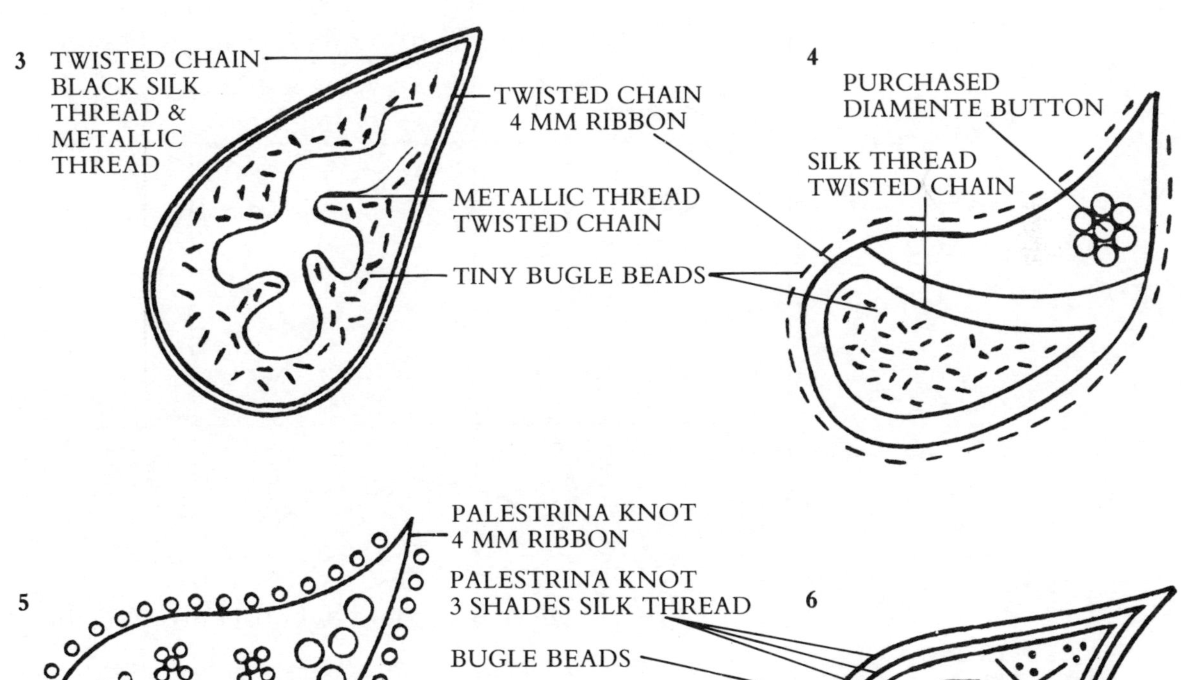

EVENING JACKET
EACH SQUARE
5×5 CM (2×2 INCHES)

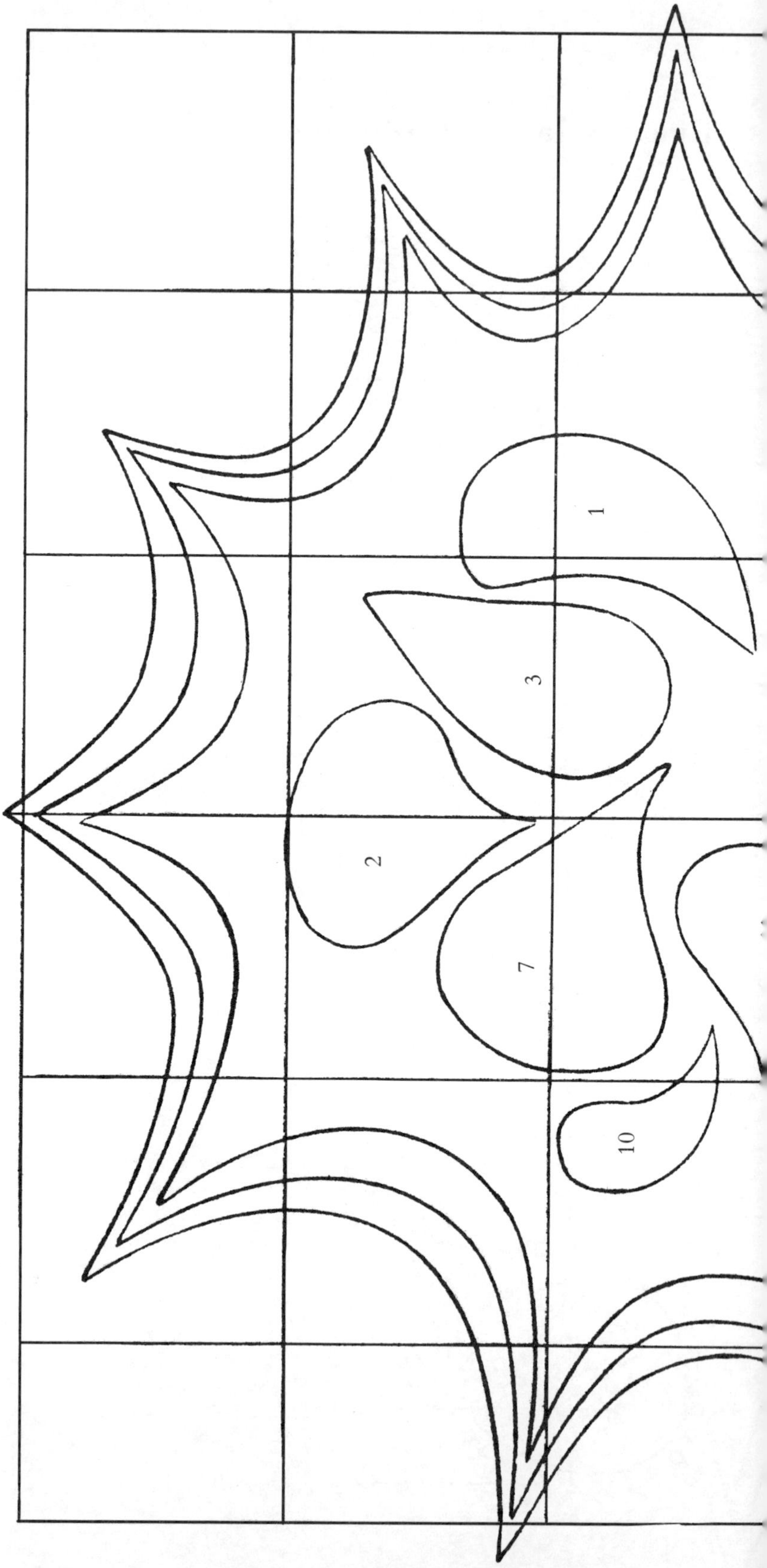

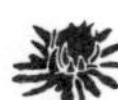

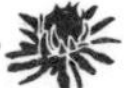

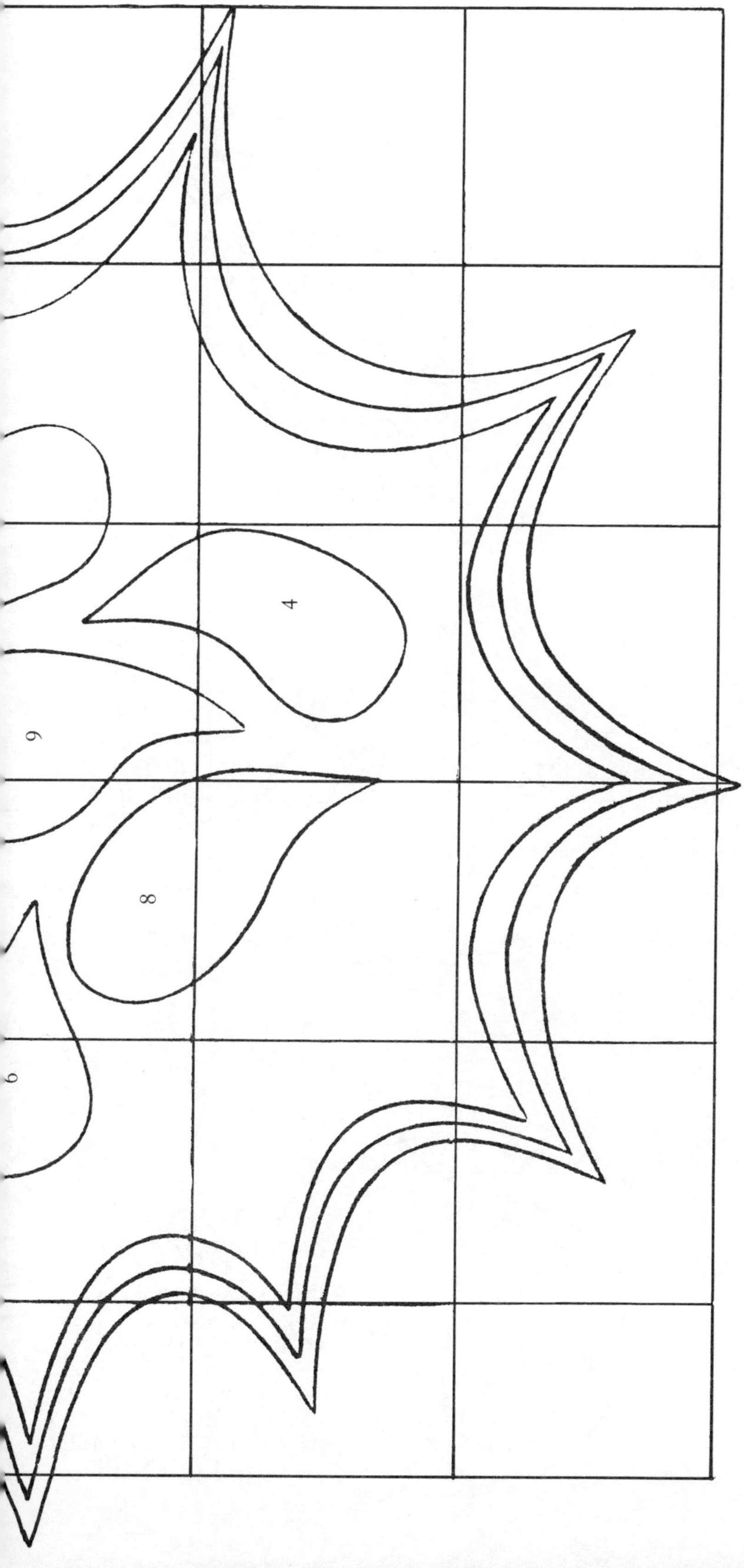

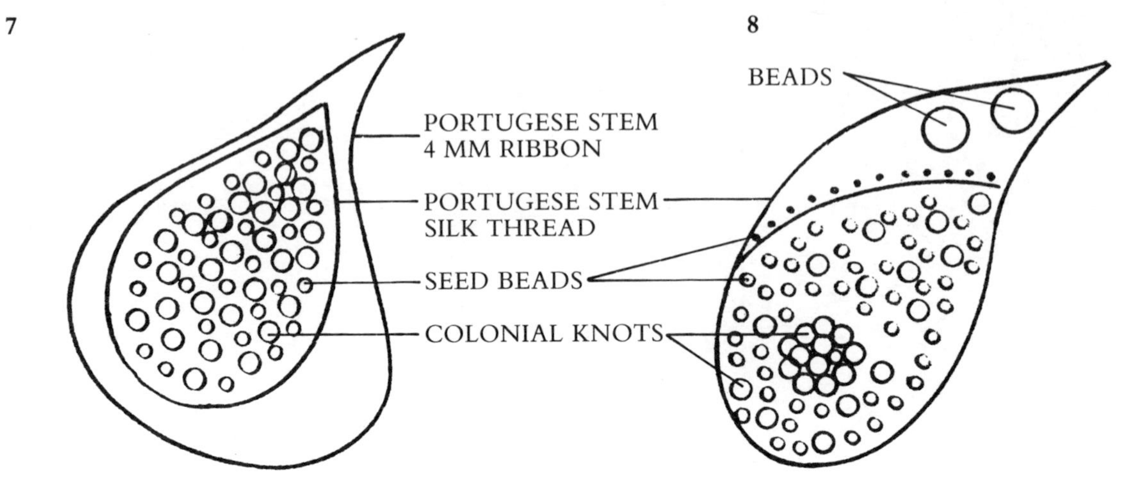

7
PORTUGESE STEM
4 MM RIBBON
PORTUGESE STEM
SILK THREAD
SEED BEADS
COLONIAL KNOTS
8
BEADS

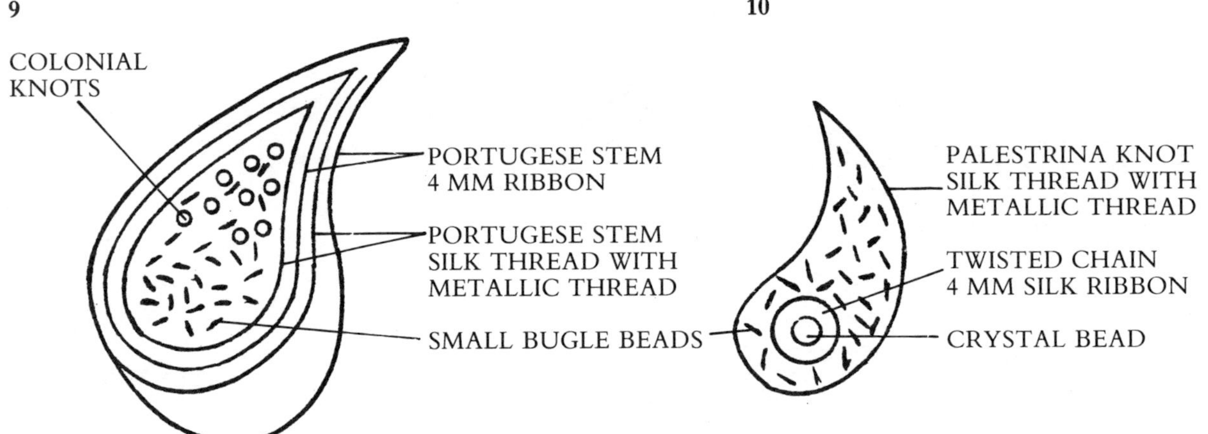

9
COLONIAL
KNOTS
PORTUGESE STEM
4 MM RIBBON
PORTUGESE STEM
SILK THREAD WITH
METALLIC THREAD
SMALL BUGLE BEADS
10
PALESTRINA KNOT
SILK THREAD WITH
METALLIC THREAD
TWISTED CHAIN
4 MM SILK RIBBON
CRYSTAL BEAD

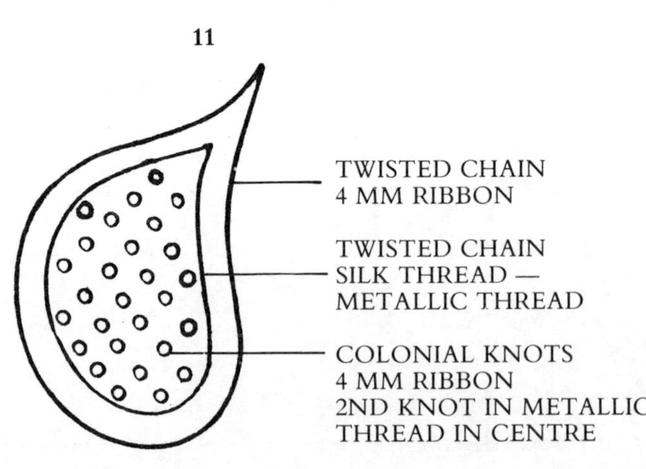

11
TWISTED CHAIN
4 MM RIBBON
TWISTED CHAIN
SILK THREAD —
METALLIC THREAD
COLONIAL KNOTS
4 MM RIBBON
2ND KNOT IN METALLIC
THREAD IN CENTRE

BELTS AND BAGS

Almost any pattern may be used and there are always several featured in the commercial dress pattern books under the heading of 'Accessories'.

These items should be stiffened sufficiently to prevent their edges rolling over. The weight of stiffening used will depend on the style selected and the weight of the original fabric. Buckram, vilene and wadding are all common recommendations, but can have some disadvantages such as deterioration over a period of time and buckram is so stiff it may be uncomfortable to wear when used in a wide belt.

Machine quilting through all thicknesses will add stiffness as will piping and/or top stitching the edges after the belt has been sewn and turned.

An excellent way of making a durable padding for belts or bags, that will not deteriorate with washing and wearing and retains flexibility, is to sandwich a piece of thin wadding between calico or flannelette and machine quilt the three layers together with very closely spaced stitching (5 mm apart). Quilt a piece of fabric slightly larger than required and then cut it to size after quilting to ensure a clean cut neat edge.

This type of stiffening is easy to sew if finishing the edges with a binding. However where it is to be used in an item that will require turning the following method may be used to avoid bulky edges.

Cut the quilted lining to the finished size (cut away the seam allowances) position and tack very carefully to the wrong side of the outside fabric section. Position and tack the lining right sides together with this section. Using a zipper foot and stitching with the quilting uppermost, stitch carefully around the edge butting the zipper foot along the edge of the quilting, but leaving an opening for turning. Turn and press very carefully. Close the opening, top stitch around the edge before removing the tacking thread that holds the quilted lining in place.

NB. top stitching must be used for this method as the lining is not held in place in any other way.

Belt

The design featured on the cummerbund style belt pictured on the back cover is reproduced below. The fabric used is lightweight polyester backed with a layer of very fine dacron wadding.

The cornelli style embroidery is worked in Portugese stem stitch in 4 mm ribbon couched with metallic thread and random areas are highlighted with colonial knots in 4 mm silk ribbon and seed beads.

The belt was constructed using the method described above, using a layer of thin batting sandwiched between two pieces of flanelette for the quilted lining.

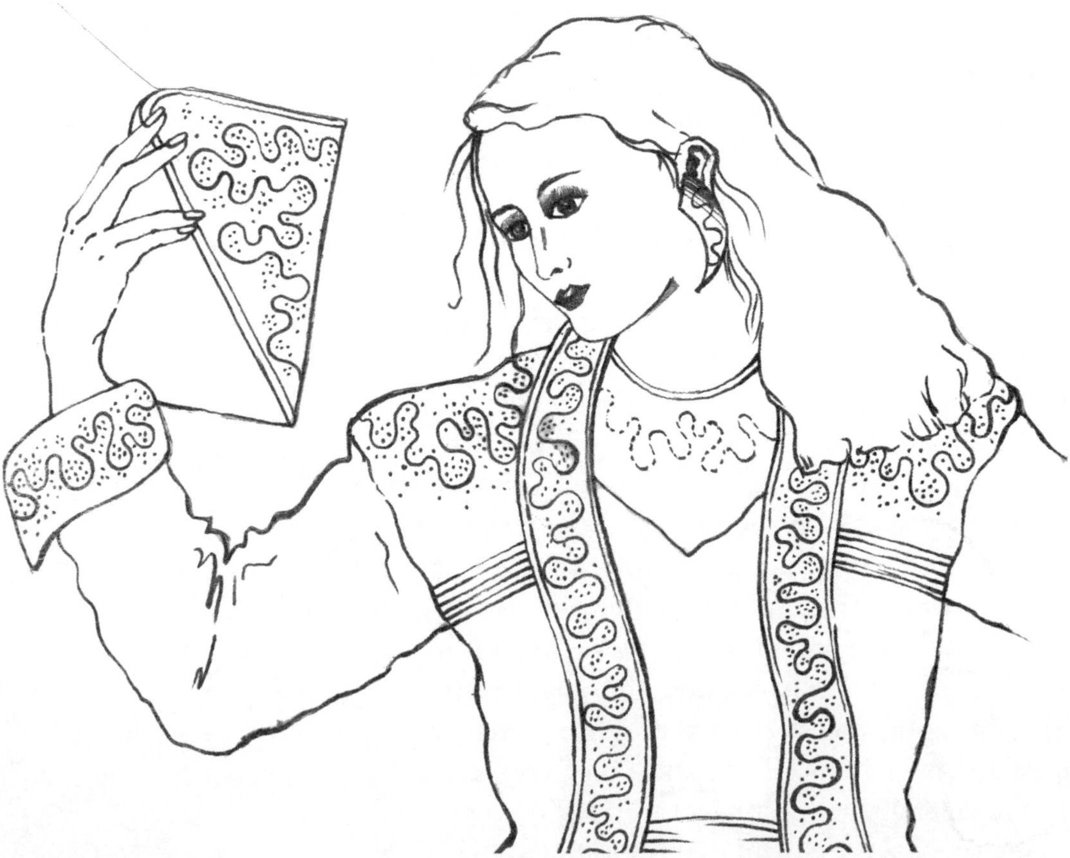

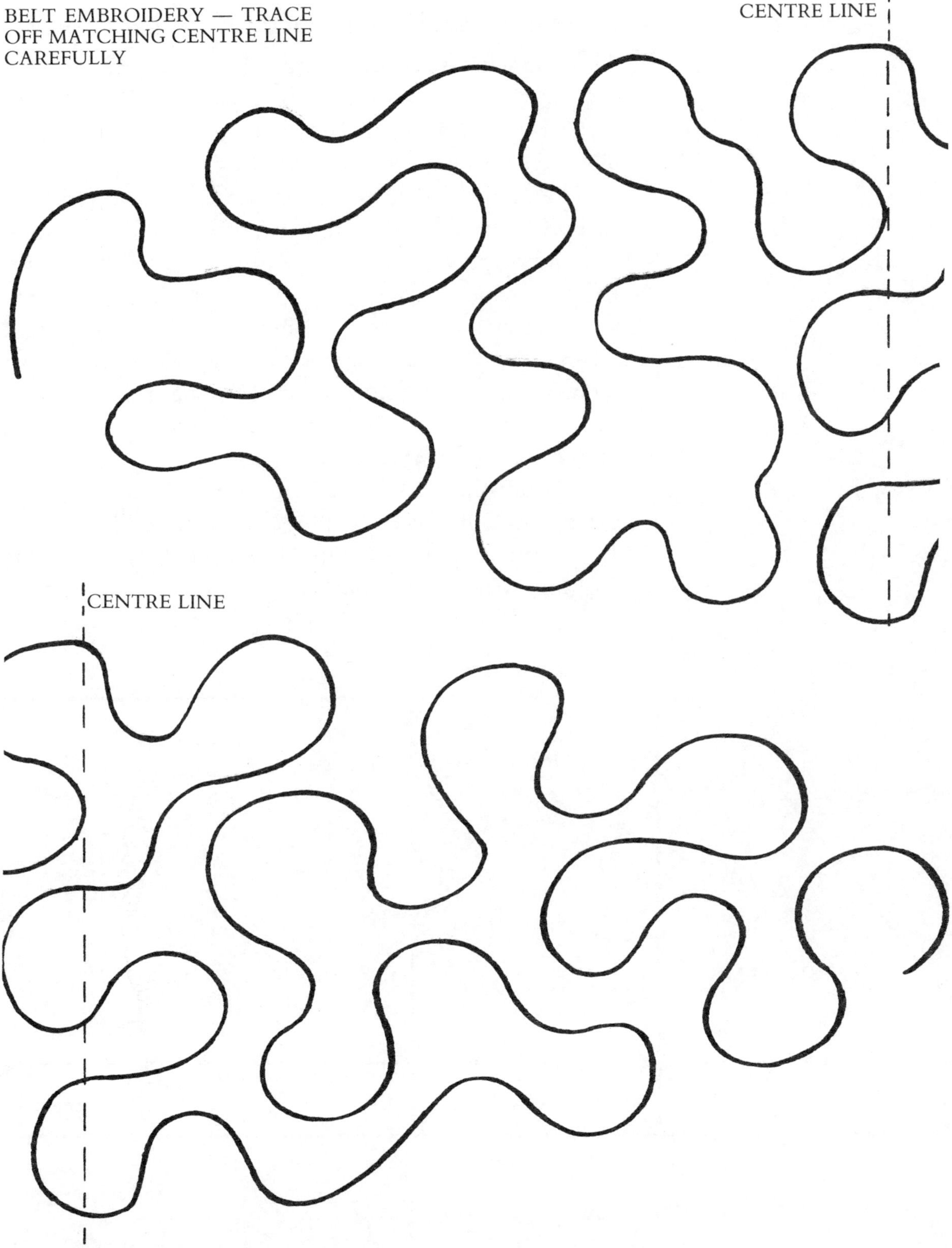

BELT EMBROIDERY — TRACE OFF MATCHING CENTRE LINE CAREFULLY

CENTRE LINE

CENTRE LINE

Envelope Style Bag (pictured on back cover)

This bag is made from a simple rectangle. The front of the bag may be shaped in a variety of ways to vary the style. I recommend curved shaping where possible to eliminate corners and make binding easier.

Pad the outside of the bag with a layer of wadding, tacking the two layers together carefully before working the embroidery, or machine quilt a piece of fabric for the bag. Cut a lining piece to match the bag section allowing an extra 2 cm (3/4 inch) on the short straight edge. Sew the two pieces together along the short straight edge right sides together using a 5 mm (3/16 inch) seam. Turn the lining to the inside over the seam allowance to form a binding.

Tack the two fabrics together, fold the bag into three, stitch the two layers together to make the pocket. Encase the raw edges with double fold braid or bias binding. Close with button and loop, press stud or Velcro tape.

ENVELOPE STYLE BAG

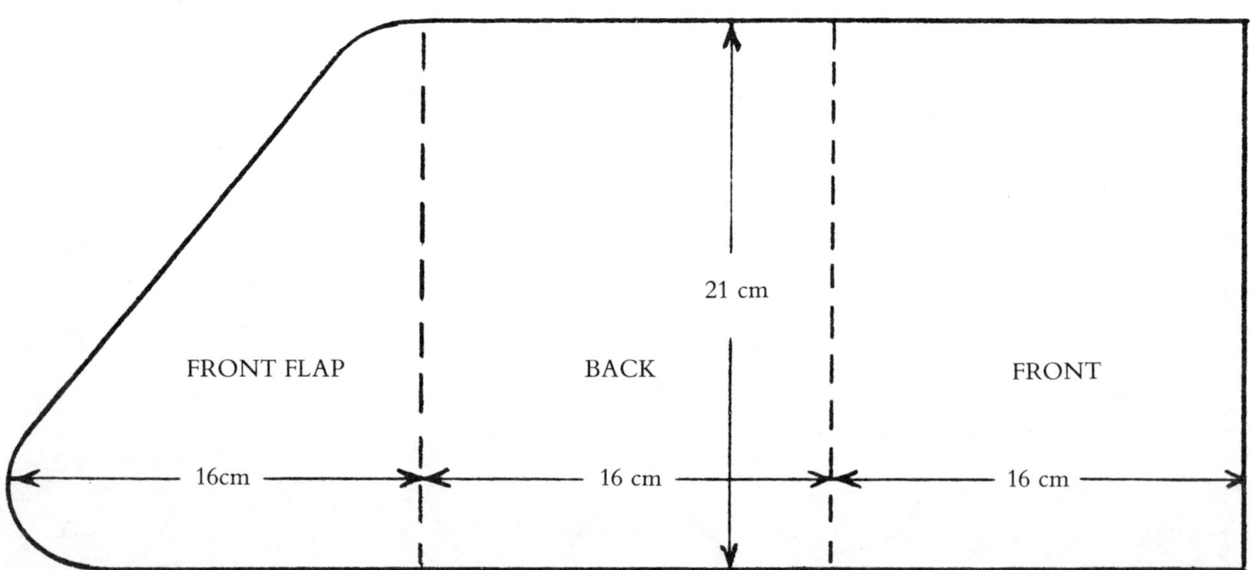

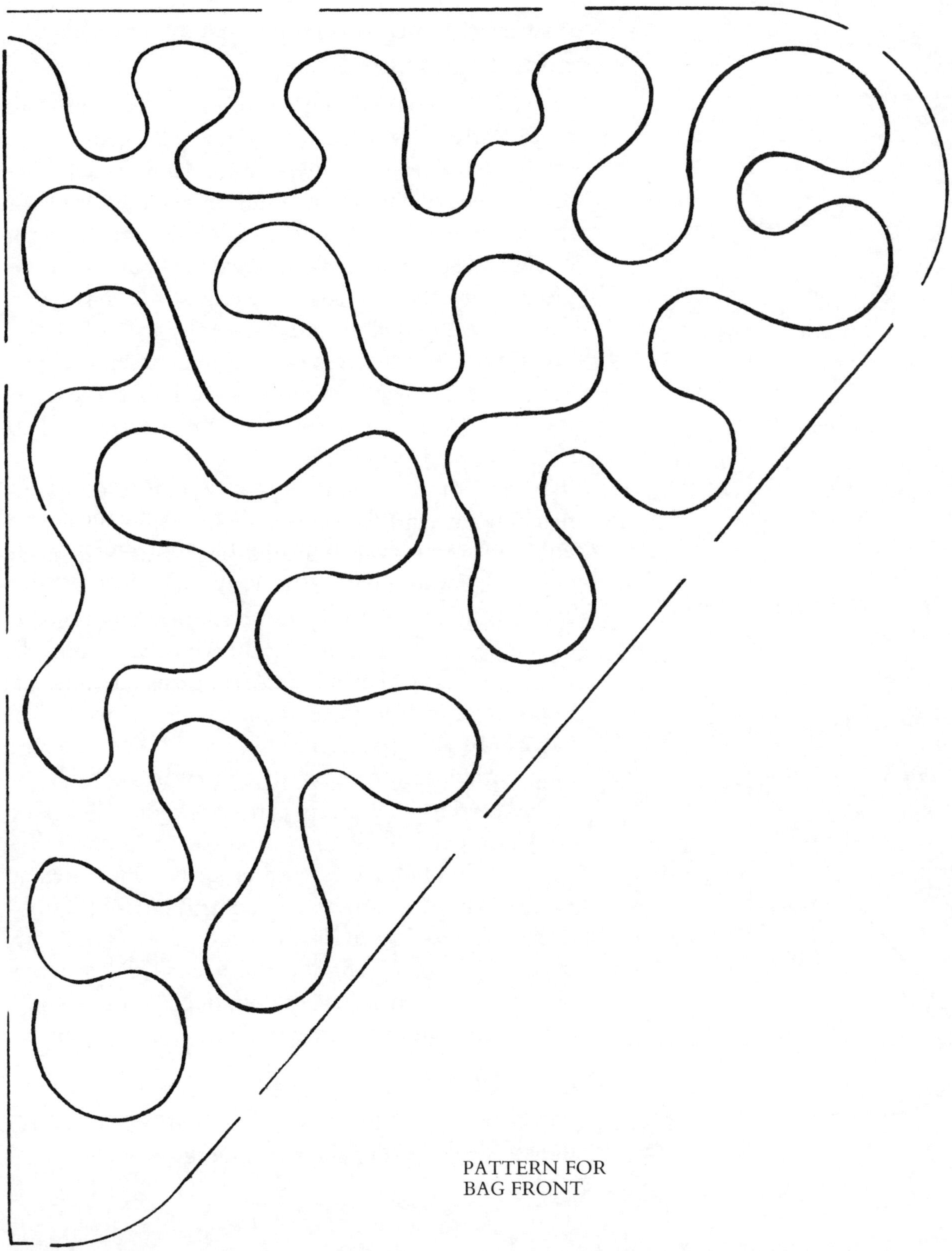

PATTERN FOR
BAG FRONT

FRONT

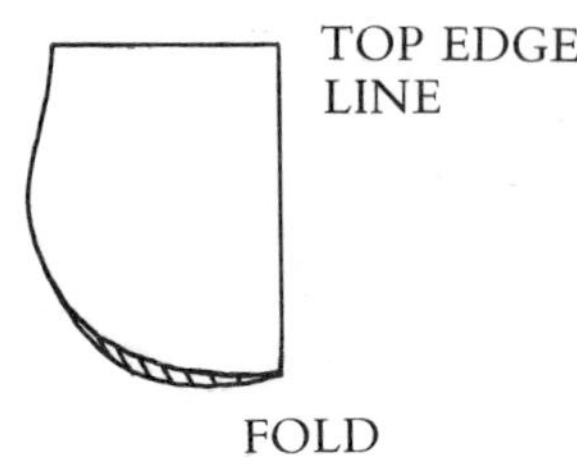

FRONT LINING AND SIMULATED FLAP

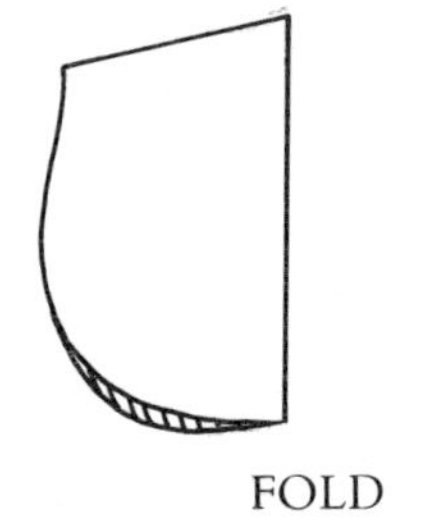

BACK INCLUDING LINING

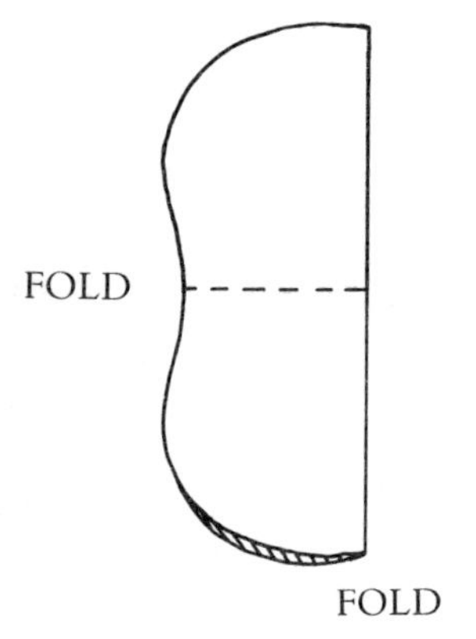

Purse Style Bag (crazy patchwork and black evening bag pictured)

- Prepare the required number of pieces from a tracing of the pattern. Note that the bag is self lined and that the back lining is cut in one piece and folded along the top edge. The front lining is extended to form the simulated flap. If you wish to use a contrasting lining and eliminate the simulated flap, cut the pattern piece along the top edge, adding seam allowances, cut out and join along the top edge.
- Work the front of the bag with the chosen design.
- Stay stitch along the seamline of the shaped edge of the front. Clip curve to stay stitching just where necessary and press under along seamline. Overlay the 'flap' onto the top of the decorated panel and machine or hand sew into place.
- Fold and press along the fold line of both sections, insert wadding if required. Tack the edges together carefully and sew front and back sections together matching top edges and having right sides outside. Cut a bias strip the required size or use double fold braid or satin bias to bind the edges carefully. The bag can be closed with a press stud fastener or a cord loop with a button covered with fabric.

Instructions for crazy patchwork may be found in books on patchwork and quilting.

When binding edges with bias cut from matching fabric that is light in weight, cut the strip and fold double. Match the raw edges with the edge of the item, sew, trim and turn folded edge to the back. Hem in place. Care must be taken to cut the binding the right width as there is no adjustment when hemming the edge.

Purse Style Bag

To make with self lining prepare two pattern pieces A and B. Then cut out the three pieces as shown.

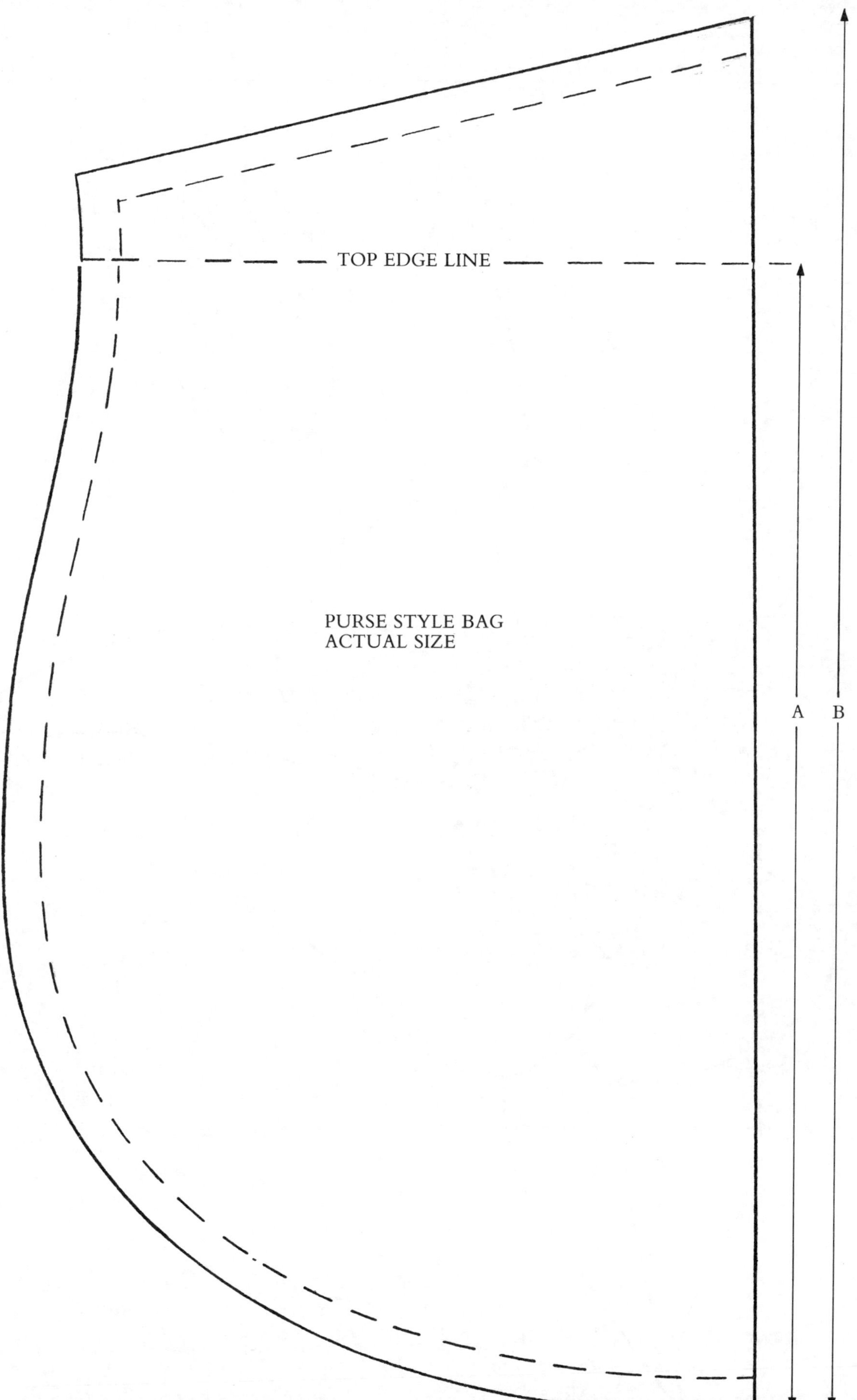
TOP EDGE LINE
PURSE STYLE BAG
ACTUAL SIZE
A
B

ROSE APPLIQUE DESIGN
ACTUAL SIZE

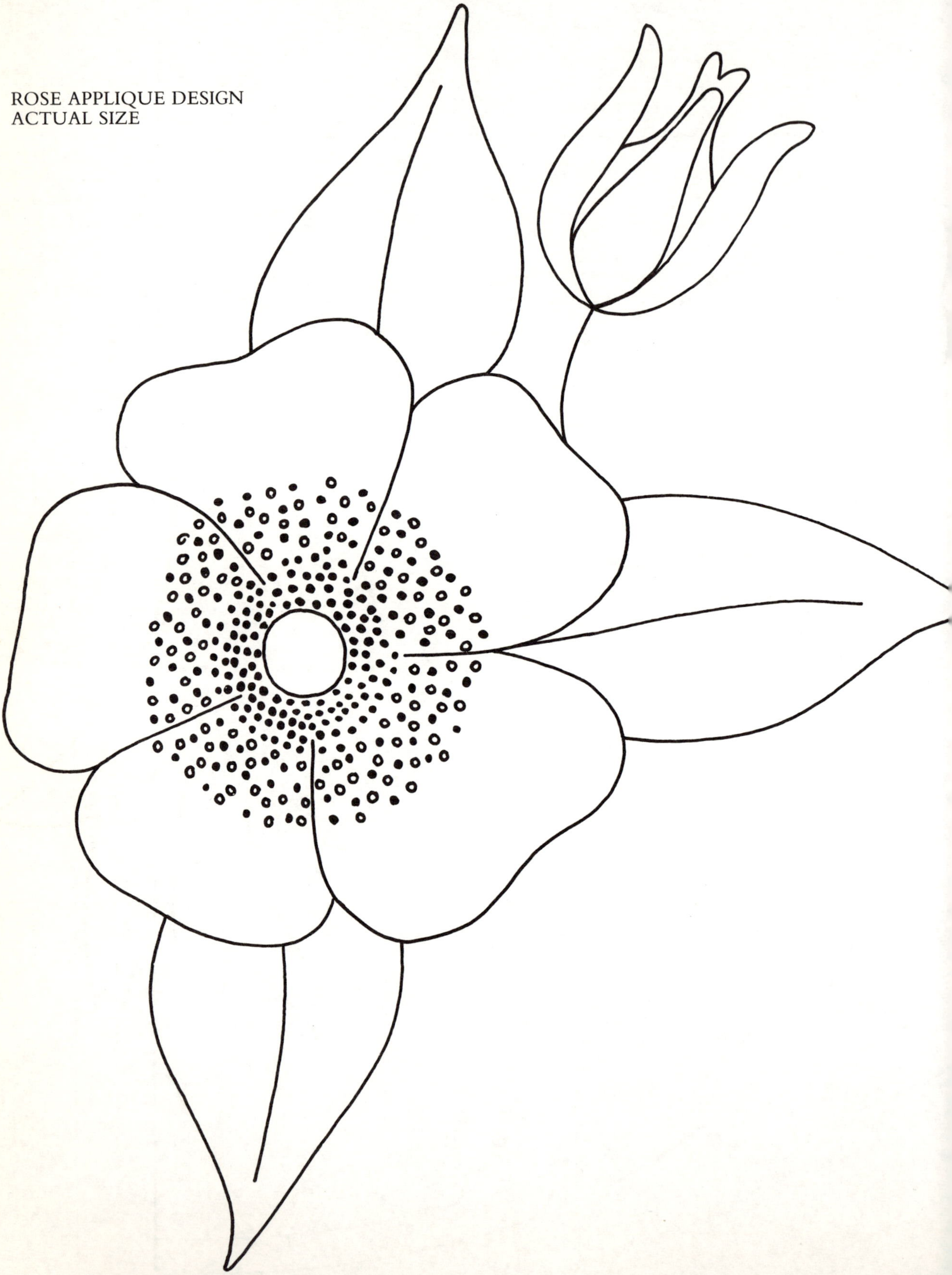

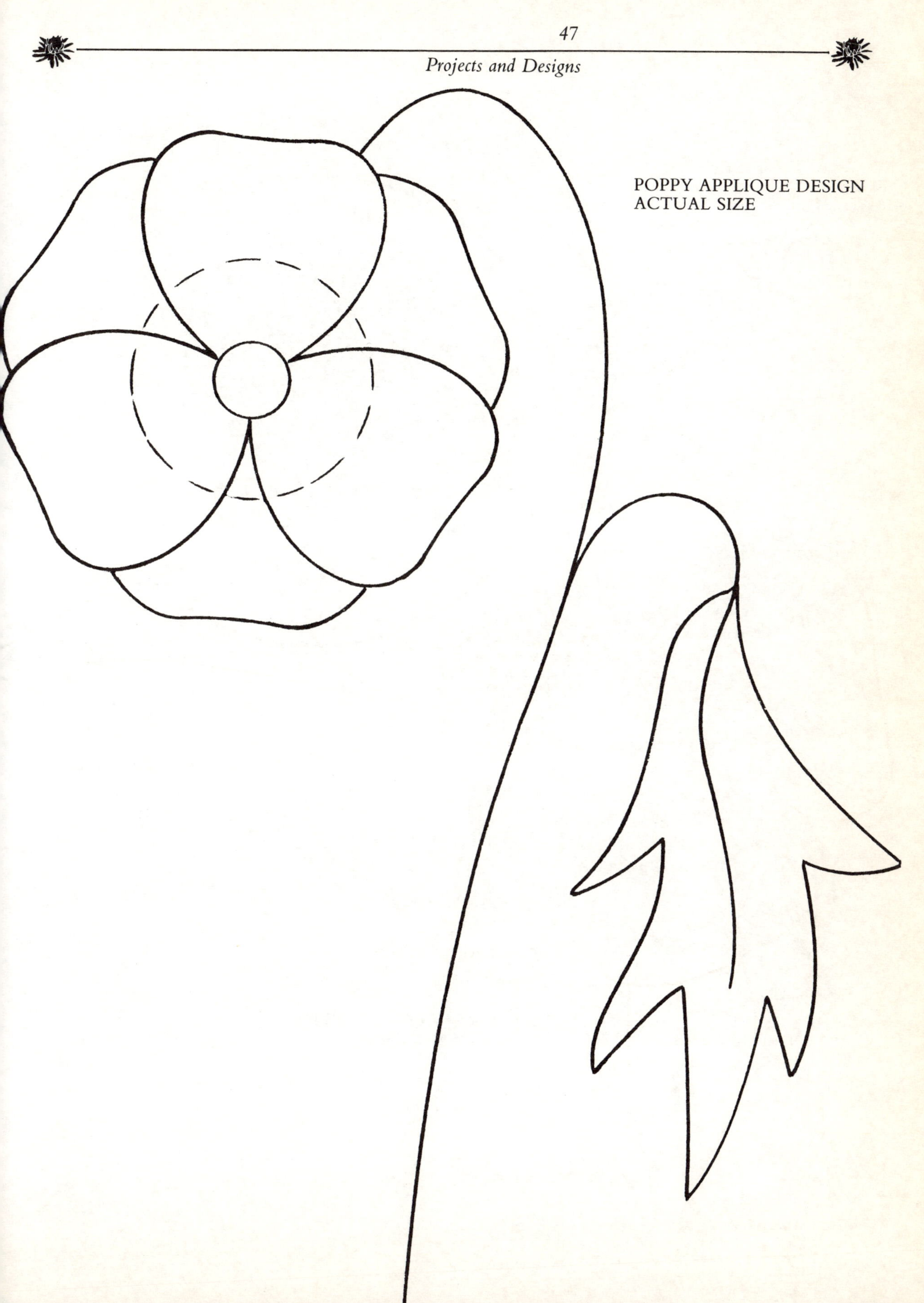
POPPY APPLIQUE DESIGN
ACTUAL SIZE

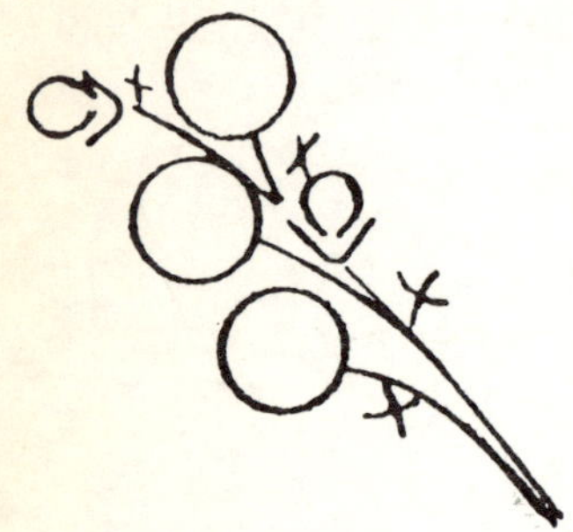

SPRAY OF ROSES

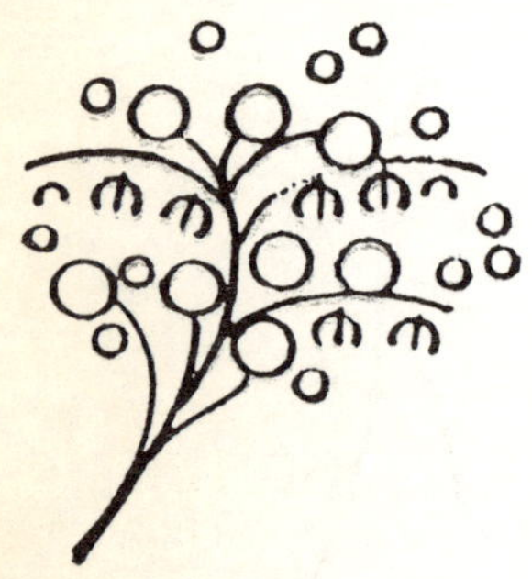

SPRAY OF
FORGET-ME-NOTS,
LILY OF THE VALLEY

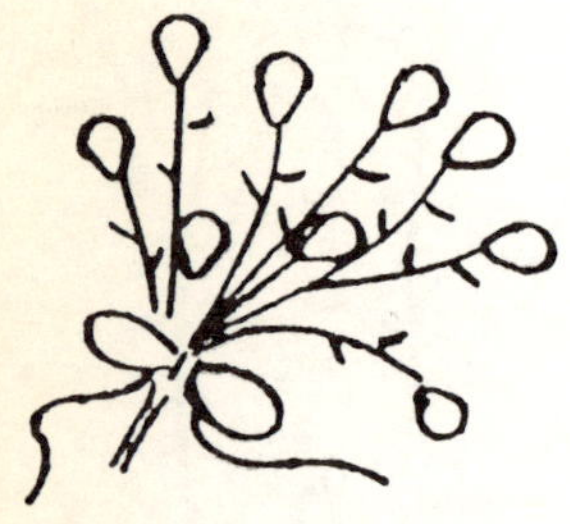

SPRAY OF ROSE BUDS

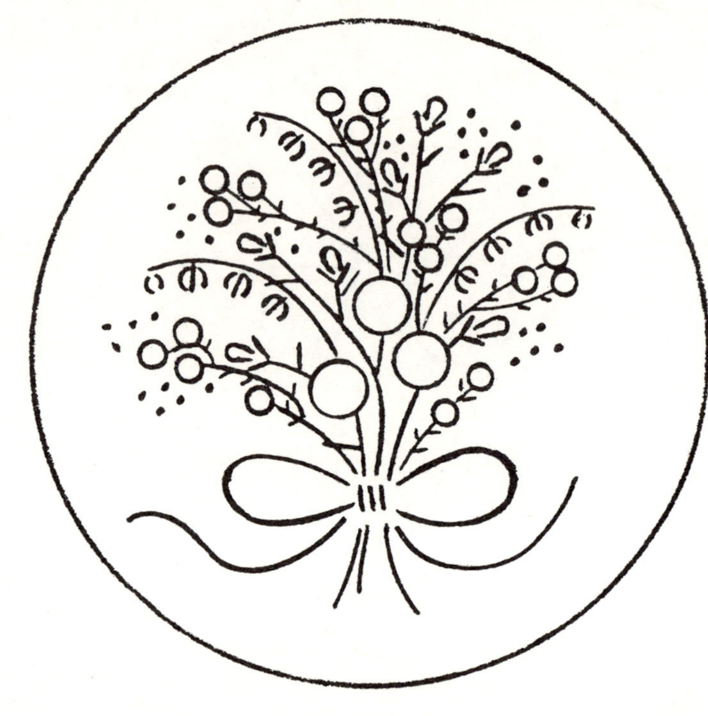

— ROSES

— FORGET ME NOTS

— LILY OF THE VALLEY

— ROSE BUDS

— BABY'S BREATH

DESIGN FOR SPRAY PICTURED
ON MIRROR BACK